CENTER FOR LANGUAGE EDUCATION AND COOPERATION
中外语言交流合作中心

暨南大学华文学院
College of Chinese Language and Culture, Jinan University

"一带一路"沿线国职业汉语系列培训教材

总主编
王衍军　林奕高　张　艳

酒店汉语

Hotel Chinese

主　编　李佳芸
副主编　林　若　滕永博　张　艳

暨南大学出版社
JINAN UNIVERSITY PRESS

中国·广州

图书在版编目（CIP）数据

酒店汉语/王衍军，林奕高，张艳总主编．—广州：暨南大学出版社，2023.12
“一带一路”沿线国职业汉语系列培训教材
ISBN 978－7－5668－3666－3

Ⅰ.①酒…　Ⅱ.①王…②林…③张…　Ⅲ.①饭店—汉语—技术培训—教材　Ⅳ.①F719.2

中国国家版本馆 CIP 数据核字（2023）第 090580 号

酒店汉语
JIUDIAN HANYU
总主编：王衍军　林奕高　张　艳

出 版 人：阳　翼
项目统筹：杜小陆
责任编辑：刘宇韬
责任校对：刘舜怡　梁玮浈
责任印制：周一丹　郑玉婷

出版发行：暨南大学出版社（511443）
电　　话：总编室（8620）37332601
营销部（8620）37332680　37332681　37332682　37332683
传　　真：（8620）37332660（办公室）　37332684（营销部）
网　　址：http://www.jnupress.com
排　　版：广州良弓广告有限公司
印　　刷：广东信源文化科技有限公司
开　　本：850mm×1168mm　1/16
印　　张：12.75
字　　数：260 千
版　　次：2023 年 12 月第 1 版
印　　次：2023 年 12 月第 1 次
定　　价：45.00 元

总 序

“一带一路”倡议的实施，为国际中文教育带来了历史机遇，在此背景下国际中文教育应主动作出调整，积极面对和适应新形势所提出的挑战。教育部在《推进共建“一带一路”教育行动》文件中强调：我们需要培养大批共建“一带一路”的急需人才，中国愿与沿线国家一道，扩大人文交流，加强人才培养，支持沿线各国实现政策互通、贸易畅通、资金融通。而语言互通则是实施“一带一路”倡议的前提和基础，国际交流与合作涉及各种途径、各个领域，需要“语言”这一重要的沟通和合作的桥梁。因此，为了“一带一路”倡议的顺利实施，特别是为推进中国与其他国家在不同职业领域的合作发展，作为汉语的母语国，中国应大力加强专门用途汉语教学。李泉教授指出：“在汉语加快走向世界的过程中，无论是基于现状还是展望未来，作为汉语的母语国都应大力推进专门用途汉语教学的发展，以满足学习者对汉语学习的多元化需求。”①

语言是交际的工具，由于某一职业领域的特殊性，该领域的从业人员自然会经常面对一些较为特殊的交际事件，因此需要了解和掌握一些与本领域有关的职业汉语词汇。比如“海关官员”和“出入境官员”面对出入境人群，自然就需要掌握一些与“出入境”相关的词语，比如“护照号、航班号、行程单、入境卡、申报、海关、签证、指纹采集、行李箱、安检处”等。这些词语在其工作中使用频率相对较高，如果他们能掌握并正确运用这些高频词语，再配合表情、动作等肢体语言，即使面对不懂外语的中国人，也基本能够进行正常的交流。

基于这样的理解和认识，我们课题组申请了中国教育部中外语言交流合作中心 2021 年度《国际中文教育中文水平等级标准》教学资源建设项目：越南、泰国、印度尼西亚《导游汉语》《警务汉语》等线上线下多模态职业汉语培训教材资源库建设项目，并成功获批，本套

① 李泉. 论专门用途汉语教学［J］. 语言文字应用，2011（3）：111.

系列教材正是该项目的研究成果。

从编写目的来看，本套系列教材主要是为“一带一路”沿线国家和地区的旅游及相关行业的从业人员提供汉语培训，提高其汉语交际能力，特别是加强这些从业人员的职业汉语技能，帮助他们更好地了解当代中国，便利这些国家和地区与中国在旅游、文化等方面的沟通与交流，提升中国人到这些国家和地区旅游观光及投资合作的吸引力，充分发挥大学服务国家战略、贴近社会生活的公共服务职能，契合“一带一路”沿线国家和地区的职业汉语需求，为民心相通、文化融合和经济发展作出深具价值的探索和贡献。

本次出版的“‘一带一路’沿线国职业汉语系列培训教材”共包含五本教材，分别是：《导游汉语》《警务汉语》《海关汉语》《酒店汉语》和《旅游局办公汉语》，因目前在境外从事导游的人员，或多或少均具有一定的汉语基础，因此《导游汉语》针对的是具备中级汉语水平的导游从业者，旨在提升其接待中国游客的汉语理解能力及跨文化交际能力。因此，该书在进行导游语言训练的同时，加强了对中国文化的介绍。通过学习和训练，他们能够更加了解中华文化，为其导游从业能力的提升打下良好的基础。而其余四本教材则针对的是汉语零基础的特定领域从业人员，如当地警察、海关官员、旅游局官员以及酒店从业者，强化和提升这些从业者在特定业务领域、特定语用场合中使用汉语沟通和交流的能力，以满足外国学习者对汉语学习的多元化需求，顺应国际中文教育在海外各职业领域蓬勃发展的时代形势。

从适用对象来看，目前出版的五本系列职业汉语教材，既可用作来华职业汉语短期培训班项目的培训教材，也可供具备初级或中级汉语水平的国内外留学生自学职业汉语。而且，为了便于学员培训和学生自学，教材编写团队为各册教材均配备了与课文内容有关的虚拟动画视频展示、每课知识点的精讲视频和教学课件以及详细的练习答案。本套系列教材多种数字化教学资源的配套呈现，既大幅降低了学员自学的学习压力，也大大减轻了培训教师的备课负担。

从编写理念来看，本套教材的编写遵循“交际性原则”，强调利用语境、场景、提问等方法使职业汉语教学交际化，因为“专门用途汉语教学”是以汉语交际为行为导向和定位目标，而不是以掌握多少汉语知识和语言点为学习目的和评价指标。在教材设计中，我们以大量听说训练来帮助学习者在短期内获得一定的职业汉语交际能力，把教学目标与特定人群在一定工作情境下的交际任务结合起来，针对性地提炼和类聚一些工作情境中所需的高频专业汉语词汇，并通过大量的课内、课外的集中操练强化对这些高频词语的理解和运用。

从教材语料来看，在语料的选取上，本套系列教材的内容力求贴近实际，贴近职业，贴近生活。为强化学习效果，我们还设计了灵活多样的练习，从机械性、有意义性到交际性的体现，各个层面都考虑到了练习形式的新颖性，而且富有可操作性和趣味性，力求最大限度调动学习者的学习能动性。除此之外，课后练习的设计还加入了一些现代化的科技元素，符合时代发展要求。

另外，需要着重说明的是，我们教材编写团队尊重图片、肖像和知识版权，教材语料来源均标明出处；教材中所下载的图片大多来源于“熊猫办公”网站。编写团队购买了“熊猫办公企业 VIP 至尊版（ID：47206601）”图片下载和使用权限，并下载了每一张图片的版权使用协议。“熊猫办公企业 VIP 至尊版”权限明确标注：图片可用于“图书出版：报纸配图、杂志封面及配图、图书封面及配图”，我们团队也保障所下载图片仅用于图书及教材配套资源出版和教学，不作他用。

除下载的图片之外，有些图片是编者所拍或所画的，均支付了相应的稿酬。有些人物图片是我们的学生和同事拍摄的，均授权我们拥有版权和使用权，我们在此特别表示感谢。此外，本套系列教材中还有极少量的图片，版权模糊，我们未能及时联络上作者。在此编者声明：图片版权归原作者所有。我们也希望作者及时联络我们，以便及时支付相应图片稿酬。

对于一些“小知识”板块的内容，我们参考了部分网站等其他材料，也均作出了一定的说明。我们尊重原作者的版权和著作权，在此也表示真诚的感谢。

总体而言，这套系列教材顺应国际中文教育的蓬勃发展趋势，具有较高的国内外推广和应用价值。当然，本套教材在很多方面还存在着不足，尽管我们在编写之初也做了某些职业领域的汉语需求调研，但各个国家汉语发展现状不同，职业汉语的需求自然也各有不同。特别是一个人的身份往往是多样的，在不同的场合有不同的身份，因此对于语言运用的需求也同样有所不同，这就导致在教材设计中很难针对某一特定人群，满足其所有的汉语交际需求。因此，这套系列教材在顶层编写设计、特定人群的汉语水平限定、教材语料内容的选取以及教材多样化练习的设计等方面均存在很多改进的余地。

我们也诚挚地欢迎国内外广大教材使用者提出宝贵的意见和修改建议，以便我们更好地修改和完善本套教材。“路漫漫其修远兮”，我们课题组不会满足于目前的五本教材，会根据国际中文市场的职业需求变化，针对更多的职业汉语需求情境，后续编写出更多的职业汉语系列教材。

教材编写组

2023 年 5 月 28 日

General Preface

The implementation of the Belt and Road Initiative has brought unprecedented opportunities for international Chinese language education. In this context, international Chinese language education should take the initiative to make adjustments and actively embrace and adapt to the challenges posed by the new situation. In the document titled *Education Action Plan for the Belt and Road Initiative*, the Ministry of Education stresses that we should cultivate the much-needed talent for the Belt and Road Initiative and China is ready to work with the countries along the routes to expand people-to-people exchanges, strengthen cooperation in the cultivation of talent, as well as support policy coordination, unimpeded trade, and financial integration among the Belt and Road countries. Language exchange is the premise and foundation for the implementation of the Belt and Road Initiative. International exchanges and cooperation involve various channels and fields, and language serves as an important bridge for communication and cooperation. Therefore, for the smooth implementation of the Belt and Road Initiative, especially for the promotion of cooperation between China and other countries in different vocational fields, China, as the native Chinese speaking country, should vigorously strengthen the teaching of Chinese for specific purposes. Professor Li Quan points out: "In the process of accelerating the Chinese language's global reach, whether based on the current situation or future prospects, China, as the native Chinese speaking country, should actively promote the development of teaching Chinese for specific purposes to meet the diverse needs of Chinese learners."①

Language is a tool for communication. Due to the particularity of some vocational field, practitioners in the field must frequently face some relatively special communicative events, and need

---

① LI Q. On teaching Chinese for specific purposes [J]. Applied linguistics, 2011 (3): 111.

to understand and master some vocational Chinese vocabulary related to the field. For example, "customs officers" and "entry-exit officers" deal with people entering and leaving the country, so naturally they need to know some words related to "entry and exit", such as "passport number, flight number, itinerary, arrival card, declaration, customs, visa, fingerprint collection, luggage, and security check", etc. These words are frequently used in their work. If they can master and use these high-frequency words correctly, together with body language such as facial expressions and gestures, basically they are able to communicate even with the Chinese people who do not know foreign languages or local languages.

Based on the above understanding, our research team applied for the 2021 Teaching Resources Construction Program of *Chinese Proficiency Grading Standards for International Chinese Language Education* supported by the Center for Language Education and Cooperation of the Ministry of Education. We proposed a project called "*Chinese for Tour Guides*, *Chinese for Police*, and other online and offline multimodal vocational Chinese training textbook resources construction project for Chinese learners in Vietnam, Thailand, and Indonesia" and it has been approved. This series of textbooks is the result of the project.

In terms of the purpose of compilation, the training textbook series mainly aims to provide Chinese language training for practitioners in tourism and related industries in countries and regions along the Belt and Road to improve their Chinese communicative competence, especially to strengthen their vocational Chinese skills, help them better understand contemporary China, facilitate the communication and exchanges between these countries and regions and China in tourism, culture and other aspects, attract more Chinese tourists and investors to these countries and regions, and give full play to the university's public service functions of serving the national strategy and getting close to social life, meet the needs of the countries and regions along the Belt and Road, make valuable exploration and contribution to people-to-people exchanges, cultural fusion and economic development.

"The Training Textbook Series of Vocational Chinese for the Countries along 'the Belt and Road'" includes five textbooks, namely, *Chinese for Tour Guides*, *Chinese for Police*, *Customs Chinese*, *Hotel Chinese*, and *Chinese for Tourism Bureau*. As most overseas tour guides currently have learned some basic Chinese, *Chinese for Tour Guides* is intended for tour guides with intermediate Chinese proficiency, aiming to enhance their Chinese comprehension and intercultural communication skills in receiving Chinese tourists. This textbook not only provides language training for tour guides, but also strengthens the introduction of Chinese culture. Through learning and training, it enables the tour guides to have a better understanding of Chinese culture and lays a good foundation for the improvement of their professional skills. The other four Chinese textbooks are aimed at practitioners in specific fields with no knowledge of Chinese language, such as local police, customs officers, tourism officials, and hotel practitioners. These textbooks aim to strengthen and improve their communication skills in Chinese in specific business fields and specific contexts, so as to meet the diversified demands of foreign Chinese learners and follow the vigorous development trend of international Chinese language education in various vocational fields overseas.

In terms of readership, the five vocational Chinese textbooks published so far in this series can not only be used as textbooks for short-term vocational Chinese training programs in China, but also be used by international students at home and abroad with primary or intermediate Chinese skills to learn vocational Chinese by themselves. Moreover, in order to facilitate the training of students and students' self-study, the textbook compilation team has equipped all textbooks with virtual animation videos, refined lecture videos and teaching courseware of the knowledge points of each lesson, as well as detailed answers for the exercises. The presentation of these various electronic supporting teaching resources not only greatly reduces the students' pressure of learning by themselves, but also frees the teachers from the burden of preparing lessons.

In terms of the compilation philosophy, this set of textbooks follows the "communicative principle", emphasizing the use of context, scene, questioning and other methods to make vocational Chinese teaching "communicative", because Chinese teaching for specific purposes takes Chinese communication as its orientation and goal, instead of regarding the mastery of Chinese knowledge and language points as its learning objective and evaluation indicator. In the textbooks, we design a large amount of listening and speaking practice to help learners acquire vocational Chinese communicative competence in a short period of time. We combine the teaching objectives with the communicative tasks of a specific group in a specific working situation, and present some high-frequency vocational Chinese words needed in the working context, and design many in-class and after-class exercises of these high-frequency words to strengthen the learners' understanding and application of them.

In terms of the selection of teaching materials, the contents of this training textbook series are close to reality, occupation, and life. Furthermore, in order to enhance learning effects, we have also designed diverse flexible exercises, from mechanical, meaningful to communicative ones. We have considered the novelty, practicability, and interest of the forms of exercises at all levels to maximize the learners' motivation. Besides, some modern technological elements have been added to the design of the after-class exercises, which is in line with the requirement of development in the new era.

In addition, we would like to stress that our textbook compilation team respects the copyright of pictures, portraits and intellectual property, and the sources of the textbook materials are cited. Most of the downloaded pictures used in the textbook are from the website "Panda Office". The compilation team has purchased the "Panda Office Enterprise VIP Supreme Edition (ID: 47206601)" to get the permission to download and use its pictures, and we have downloaded the copyright and use agreement for each picture as well. "Panda Office Enterprise VIP Supreme Edition" clearly indicates the permission that pictures can be used for "book publication: newspaper illustrations, magazine covers and illustrations, book covers and illustrations". Our team also guarantees that the downloaded pictures will only be used in the textbooks and relevant multimedia resources, and will not be used for other purposes.

Apart from the downloaded images, there are some pictures taken or drawn by the compilers and the corresponding remuneration has been paid. Some pictures of the characters are taken by our students and colleagues, who agree that we hold the copyrights and the right to use them, for which we would like to express our special thanks. There are also a very small number of images in this series with ambiguous copyrights, and we were unable to contact the authors in time. The compilers hereby declare that the copyrights of these pictures belong to the original authors. We also hope that the authors will contact us so that we can pay the corresponding remuneration.

For the contents of some of the "Notes" sections, we have referred to some websites and other materials, and have also cited the publications and their sources. We respect the copyright of the original authors and would like to express our sincere gratitude here.

In general, this training textbook series has come out in response to the vigorous development of international Chinese education, and has high promotion and application value at home and abroad. Undoubtedly, this training textbook series still has shortcomings in many aspects. For example, although we conducted research on the demand for Chinese language learning in certain vocational fields at the beginning of the compilation, the current development status of Chinese language varies in different countries, and the demand for vocational Chinese learning naturally varies. Especially since a person's identity varies on different occasions, one's needs for language use are also different. There fore, it is difficult for the training textbook series to meet all the demands of a specific group. Therefore, there is still room for improvement for this training textbook series in terms of top-level compilation design, the limitation of the Chinese proficiency for specific groups, the selection of teaching contents and the design of diversified exercises.

We also sincerely welcome valuable comments and suggestions from the users of the textbooks at home and abroad, so that we can better modify and improve this training textbook series. "There is still a long way to go", our team will not be content with the current five textbooks, but will follow up with more series of vocational Chinese textbooks based on the changing vocational needs of the international Chinese market, targeting more vocational Chinese language demand scenarios.

Textbook Writing Group

28th May, 2023

前言

《酒店汉语》是为实施“一带一路”沿线国家汉语培训项目所编写的职业汉语系列教材之一。随着中国境外旅游人数逐年增多，许多境外酒店都需要能使用汉语进行沟通和服务的工作人员，而汉语水平能够与中国游客顺利沟通也是酒店从业者获得较高待遇的重要技能之一。

本教材中所说的“酒店汉语”，是指酒店从业者为入住酒店的客人提供住宿服务过程中所使用的汉语，属于专门用途汉语之一。目前国内与“酒店汉语”相关的学习内容大多与“旅游汉语”或“商务汉语”等方面的教材相融合，而且相关教材的适用对象主要为来华旅游和对中国文化感兴趣的外国人，编写目的是帮助其提高汉语水平。作为一门专业性较强的职业技能，酒店汉语教材的编写需要明确教学内容、范围和对象，注重实践性和操作性，使学习者能够将所学内容运用于酒店服务工作之中。

本教材的编写目的，主要是为帮助国外酒店工作人员了解当代中国概况，掌握酒店服务工作流程中的汉语交际用语，掌握酒店专业词汇和特定的表达方式，并能与中国游客进行日常口语和交际会话。

本教材在需求调查结果的基础上，以汉语教材编写的一般性原则为指导，参考上海师范大学对外汉语学院旅游汉语功能大纲课题组编著的《旅游汉语功能大纲》中“饭店实务”的情景条目，设置了四个教学模块，内容涵盖问询接待、餐厅、客房和康体等酒店一线工作中的服务内容。各个课程模块根据实际工作场景来设计学习任务，课文内容涉及咨询、入住、订餐、送餐、打扫、洗衣服务、运动健身、游泳、按摩等跟酒店客人密切相关的汉语知识和交际用语。每一课在教学任务完成后，均搭配多种类型的交际练习，课后练习在设计上以听力和口语交际为主，以便学习者在酒店的从业环境中学以致用。

本教材从汉语拼音讲起，简单介绍了汉语中的声母、韵母和声调等入门知识，适合具有初级汉语水平的酒店从业人员使用，同时也可以作为旅游从业人员的培训教材。

李佳芸　林　若

2023 年 6 月 28 日

Preface

Hotel Chinese is one of the vocational Chinese textbooks developed for the implementation of the "Maritime Silk Road" Chinese training program. As the number of Chinese tourists abroad increases year by year, many overseas hotels need staff who can communicate and serve in Chinese. Being able to speak Chinese and communicate smoothly with Chinese tourists is also one of the important skills for hotel practitioners to obtain higher treatment.

The term "Hotel Chinese" in this textbook refers to the Chinese language used by hotel practitioners in the process of providing accommodation services for hotel guests, which belongs to "Chinese for Specific Purposes". At present, most of the learning contents related to "Hotel Chinese" in China are integrated with the textbooks for "Tourism Chinese" and "Business Chinese", and these textbooks are mainly intended for foreigners who are traveling in China and are interested in Chinese culture, with the purpose of helping them improve their Chinese proficiency. To cultivate the professional skill, the compilation of hotel Chinese teaching materials needs to clarify the teaching content, scope and object, and pay attention to practicality and operability, so that learners can apply what they have learned to the hotel service work.

The textbook aims to help foreign hotel staff gain an overview of contemporary China, master the Chinese language used for communication in the hotel service work process, command the professional vocabulary and specific expressions in hotel service, and conduct daily communicative conversations with Chinese tourists.

Based on the results of the demand survey, this textbook is guided by the general principles of compiling Chinese language textbooks. With reference to the scenario items of "Hotel Practice" in the *Tourism Chinese Functional Syllabus* compiled by the Research Group of Tourism Chinese

Functional Syllabus of the International College of Chinese Studies of Shanghai Normal University, four teaching modules are set up, covering the contents of the front – line hotel services of reception, restaurant, room service department and recreation. The learning task of each module is designed according to the actual working scenarios. The texts cover Chinese knowledge and communicative terms closely related to hotel guests, such as inquiry, checking in, ordering, food delivery, cleaning, laundry service, sports and fitness, swimming, massage, etc. Each unit is equipped with various types of communicative exercises after the teaching task. The after-class exercises focus on listening and oral communication, so that learners can apply what they have learned in their working environment.

This textbook starts with Chinese pinyin and introduces the basic knowledge of initial consonants, finals and tones in Chinese. It is suitable for hotel practitioners with primary Chinese level and can also be used as a training textbook for tourism practitioners.

Li Jiayun, Lin Ruo

28th June, 2023

Hotel Chinese
酒店汉语

目　录
Contents

汉语入门

一

拼音

汉语的音节大多数由声母、韵母和声调三部分组成。音节开头的辅音叫声母，声母后面的音节叫韵母。声调指音节中具有区别意义作用的音高变化。现代汉语普通话有 400 多个声韵组合，1200 多个音节。

Most Chinese syllables are composed of initials, finals and tones. The consonant at the head of a syllable is called initial, the rest of the syllable is the final. The different pitches that distinguish words from others are called tones. The contemporary Mandarin Chinese has more than 400 initial-final combinations and over 1200 syllables.

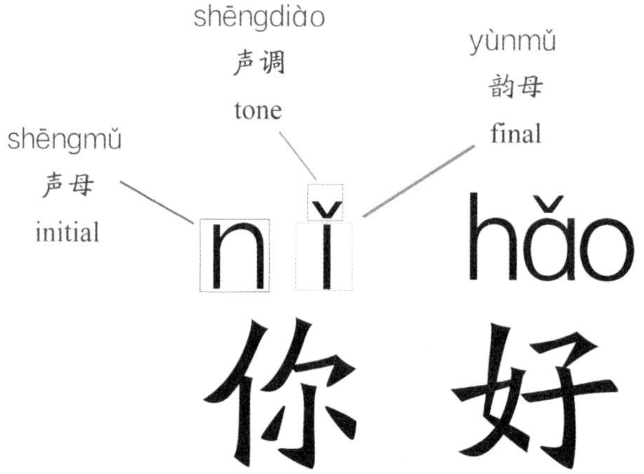

声母、韵母和声调 Initials, Finals and Tones

现代汉语普通话里有 21 个辅音声母，39 个韵母，4 个声调。

There are 21 consonant initials, 39 finals and 4 tones in the contemporary Mandarin Chinese.

声母 Initials

b	p	m	f
d	t	n	l
g	k	h	
z	c	s	
zh	ch	sh	r
j	q	x	
Note：zero initials：y w			

韵母 Finals

a o e i u ü
ai ei ao ou
an ang en eng ong
ia ie iao i（o）u ian in iang ing
üe üan ün iong
ua uo uai ui（uei） uan un（uen） uang ueng
－i（zi ci si） －i（zhi chi shi ri） er ê

声调　Tones

现代汉语普通话里有四个基本声调：第一声、第二声、第三声、第四声，分别使用声调符号：ˉ（第一声）、ˊ（第二声）、ˇ（第三声）、ˋ（第四声）。

There are 4 basic tones in the contemporary Mandarin Chinese. They are shown by the tone marks：ˉ（the first tone）、ˊ（the second tone）、ˇ（the third tone）、ˋ（the fourth tone）.

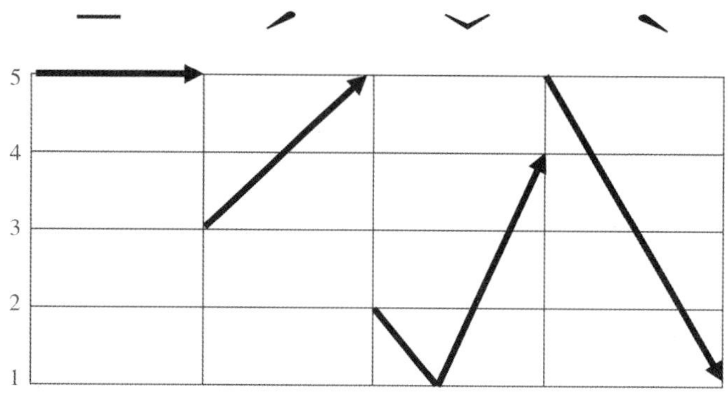

汉语里的声调具有区别意义的作用，声调不同，表达的意义则不同。例如：

The tones in Chinese have the function of distinguishing meanings. Different tones may express different meanings. E. g. ,

 妈 mā	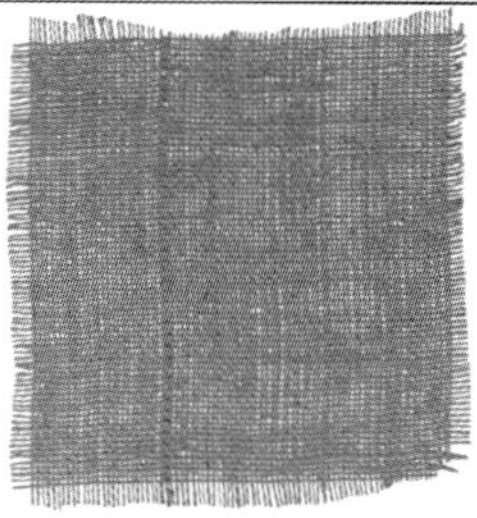 麻 má	 马 mǎ	 骂 mà

拼音书写规则　Rules of Spelling Pinyin

1. 声调标在韵母（主要元音）上，不标在声母上。

The tone marks should be placed over the finals (main vowels), rather than the initials.

2. 标调的顺序是“ɑ > o > e > i > u > ü”。

The order of tone mark placement is “ɑ > o > e > i > u > ü”.

hǎo	dōu	féi	hái	lüè

3. “i”“u”同时出现时，声调标在最后一个元音上。

When “i” and “u” appear together, tone mark should be placed over the last vowel.

liù	qiú	jiǔ	guì	duì

4. 声调标在“i”上时，“i”上的点需要省略。

The dot over “i” should be removed when the tone mark is put over “i”.

dì	mǐ	huī	kuì	tuì

5. “i”“u”“ü”可以自成音节。自成音节时，分别写成“yi”“wu”“yu”。

“i”, “u”, and “ü” can form syllables by themselves. When they form their own syllables, they are written as “yi”, “wu”, and “yu” respectively.

	→	
i		yi
u		wu
ü		yu

以“i”开头的音节，“i”要写成“y”。以“ü”开头的音节，音节开头要加上“y”，“ü”上面的两点要去掉。以“u”开头的音节，“u”要写成“w”。

“i” at the beginning of a syllable is written as “y”. “y” is added before the syllable beginning with “ü”, and the two dots over “ü” are removed. “u” at the beginning of a syllable is written as “w”.

	→	
ia iao iou		ya yao you
üe üan ün		yue yuan yun
ua uai uo uei		wa wai wo wei

6. “ü” “üe” “üan” “ün” 和 “j” “q” “x” “y” 相拼时，“ü” 上面的两点要去掉。

When “ü”, “üe”, “üan” or “ün” is spelled together with “j”, “q”, “x”, or “y”, the two dots at the top of “ü” should be removed.

jú	qù	xué	xuán	yūn

轻声 The Neutral Tone

汉语中有些音节不加声调（无论它们所代表的汉字是第几声），读得很轻、很短，这样的音节叫轻声。轻声音高受前面一个音节声调的影响而变化。例如：

Some syllables in Chinese are toneless (disregarding the tones of the characters they represent) and are pronounced light and short. These syllables are called neutralized tones or neutral tones. The pitch of a neutral tone is affected by the tone of the preceding syllable. E. g.,

dìdi 弟弟 younger brother	wǒmen 我们 we, us	hǎo de 好 的 well, OK	péngyou 朋友 friend

注意：在拼写中，轻声音节不标调号。

Note: In transcription, neutral tones don't carry any tone marks.

“er” 和儿化韵 The Retroflex “er” and the R-ending Finals

1. 发“er”时，先把舌位放到发“e”的位置，然后将舌尖轻轻上翘，同时发音。例如：

To pronounce “er”, first put the tongue in the position for “e”, and then slightly curl up the tip of the tongue. E. g. ,

érgē 儿歌 nursery rhyme	érnǚ 儿女 sons and daughters, children	ěrduo 耳朵 ear	èrshí 二十 twenty

2. “er”可以与其他的韵母组合成一个儿化韵。儿化韵的写法是在原韵母后面加“r”，汉字写法是在原汉字后面加个“儿”字（有时候也可以省略，不用写）。例如：

The final “er” can be combined with another final to form a r-ending final. In transcription it is shown by adding a “r” to the original final. When writing the Chinese character, we add “儿” after the original character (sometimes it can be omitted). E. g. ,

huār 花儿 flower	wánr 玩儿 to play	yǒudiǎnr 有点儿 a little	zhèr 这儿 here

隔音符号　The Syllable-dividing Mark

以“a”“o”“e”开头的音节连接在其他音节后面的时候，如果音节的界限发生混淆，用隔音符号（’）隔开。例如：

When a syllable beginning with “a”, “o”, and “e” follows another syllable, it is desirable to use a dividing-mark (’) to clarify the boundary between the two syllables. E. g. ,

bǎo’ ān　保安

变调　Tone Sandhi

两个第三声音节连读时，前一个音节要读成第二声。例如：

When a 3rd tone is immediately followed by another 3rd tone, the former syllable is pronounced as the 2nd tone. E. g. ,

nǐ hǎo ⇨ ní hǎo　你好

yǔsǎn ⇨ yúsǎn　雨伞

音节和汉字　Syllables and Chinese Characters

汉字是记录汉语的书写符号系统。一个音节可以转换为一个或若干个汉字。例如：

Chinese characters are a system of written symbols that records the Chinese language. One syllable can represent one or several characters. E. g. ,

nán 男 male	nǚ 女 female	dà 大 big	xiǎo 小 small

二

基本数字

1	一	yī	数	one
2	二	èr	数	two
3	三	sān	数	three
4	四	sì	数	four
5	五	wǔ	数	five
6	六	liù	数	six
7	七	qī	数	seven
8	八	bā	数	eight
9	九	jiǔ	数	nine
10	十	shí	数	ten
11	百	bǎi	数	hundred
12	千	qiān	数	thousand
13	万	wàn	数	ten thousand
14	百万	bǎiwàn	数	million
15	亿	yì	数	hundred million

三

基本称呼

1	爸爸	bàba	名	father，dad
2	妈妈	māma	名	mother，mom
3	哥哥	gēge	名	elder brother
4	姐姐	jiějie	名	elder sister
5	弟弟	dìdi	名	younger brother
6	妹妹	mèimei	名	younger sister
7	爷爷	yéye	名	grandfather（father's father）
8	奶奶	nǎinai	名	grandmother（father's mother）
9	外公	wàigōng	名	grandfather（mother's father）
10	外婆	wàipó	名	grandmother（mother's mother）
11	叔叔	shūshu	名	uncle（father's younger brother）
12	伯伯	bóbo	名	uncle（father's elder brother）
13	舅舅	jiùjiu	名	uncle（mother's brother）
14	阿姨	āyí	名	aunt（mother's sister）
15	姨妈	yímā	名	aunt（mother's sister）
16	姑姑	gūgu	名	aunt（father's sister）
17	姑妈	gūmā	名	aunt（father's sister）

四

基本词语

1	我	wǒ	代	I, me
2	你	nǐ	代	you (singular)
3	您	nín	代	you (honorific)
4	他	tā	代	he, him
5	她	tā	代	she, her
6	们	men	后缀	plural marker for pronouns and nouns
7	这	zhè	代	this
8	那	nà	代	that
9	请	qǐng	动	please
10	进	jìn	动	to come in
11	坐	zuò	动	to sit
12	呢	ne	助	a modal particle used at the end of a sentence
13	吗	ma	助	a modal particle used at the end of a question
14	吧	ba	助	a modal particle used at the end of a sentence

15	早上	zǎoshang	名	early morning
16	上午	shàngwǔ	名	morning
17	下午	xiàwǔ	名	afternoon
18	晚上	wǎnshang	名	evening
19	欢迎	huānyíng	动	to welcome

五

基本会话

Nǐ hǎo! A：你 好！ Nǐ hǎo! B：你 好！	
Lǎoshī, nín hǎo! A：老师， 您 好！ Nǐ hǎo! B：你 好！	
Xièxie! A：谢谢！ Bú kèqi。/ Búyòng xiè。 B：不 客气。/ 不用 谢。	
Duìbuqǐ! A：对不起！ Méi guānxi。 B：没 关系。	
Zàijiàn! A：再见！ Zàijiàn! B：再见！	

你知道吗

中国人如何打招呼?

中国人初次见面，一般说“您好”或“你好”！也可根据见面的时间，说“早上好”“下午好”或“晚上好”等。而朋友之间打招呼则较为灵活，可以说：“干什么去?”或者对方正在做什么，就问什么，比如看见对方正在吃饭，可以说：“在吃饭呢?”

这种打招呼的方式一般表示“我看到你了，跟你打个招呼”，并不要求对方回答什么。

How do Chinese People Greet Each Other?

When Chinese people meet each other for the first time, they usually say “您好” or “你好”. They may also say “早上好 (Good morning)”, “下午好 (Good afternoon)” or “晚上好 (Good evening)”, depending on the time they meet. Friends are more casual in greeting each other. One can say: “干什么去? (What are you going to do?)” Or they can ask what the other party is doing. For example, when seeing a friend having dinner, one may say: “在吃晚饭呢? (Having dinner?)”

This way of greeting generally means “hello” rather than an actual question, and does not require any answer.

第一课

您好！请问有什么可以帮您

课前热身 Warming up

1. 你知道怎么预订酒店吗？

   Do you know how to book a hotel room?

2. 网上预订酒店需要哪些预订信息？

   What booking information is required for online hotel reservations?

课文 Text

中国商人李伟下星期要去曼谷出差，他要预订玫瑰酒店（Rose Hotel）的一间单人房，他打电话到酒店前台询问。

Li Wei, who is on a business trip to Bangkok, wants to book a single room at the Rose Hotel. He calls the front desk to make a reservation.

Lǐ Wěi
李 伟

中国商人

A business man from China

fúwùyuán
服务员

酒店前台

a waitress at the front desk

Fúwùyuán： Nín hǎo！ Zhèlǐ shì Méigui Jiǔdiàn， Qǐngwèn yǒu shénme kěyǐ
服务员：您 好！这里 是 玫瑰 酒店， 请问 有 什么 可以

bāng nín?
帮 您？

Lǐ Wěi： Nín hǎo! Wǒ yào yùdìng yí gè fángjiān。
李 伟：您 好！我 要 预订 一个 房间。

Fúwùyuán： Hǎo de， xiānsheng。 Qǐngwèn nín yào yùdìng jǐ hào de fángjiān?
服务员：好 的， 先生 。 请问 您 要 预订 几号 的 房间？

Lǐ Wěi： yuè hào。
李 伟： 7 月 18 号。

Fúwùyuán: Hǎo de, Qǐngwèn nín yào dān rén jiān háishi shuāng rén jiān?
服务员：好的，请问您要单人间还是双人间？

Lǐ Wěi: Dān rén jiān。Duōshao qián yìtiān? Yǒu zǎocān ma?
李伟：单人间。多少钱一天？有早餐吗？

Fúwùyuán: Dān rén jiān yìtiān měiyuán, yǒu zǎocān。Qǐngwèn nín yào zhù jǐ tiān?
服务员：单人间一天88美元，有早餐。请问您要住几天？

Lǐ Wěi: Zhù sān tiān。
李伟：住三天。

Fúwùyuán: Hǎo de, xiānsheng。Nín yùdìng de shì yuè hào dào hàode dān rén jiān, měiyuán yìtiān, yǒu zǎocān。Qǐng nín quèrèn yíxià。
服务员：好的，先生。您预订的是7月18号到21号的单人间，88美元一天，有早餐。请您确认一下。

Lǐ Wěi: Duì de。
李伟：对的。

Fúwùyuán: Qǐng gàosu wǒ nín de xìngmíng、hùzhào hàomǎ hé yóuxiāng。
服务员：请告诉我您的姓名、护照号码和邮箱。

Lǐ Wěi: Wǒ jiào LǐWěi, hùzhào hàomǎ shì yóuxiāng shì
李伟：我叫李伟，护照号码是CN7832，邮箱是liwei@163. com。

Fúwùyuán: Lǐ xiānsheng, nín de fángjiān yùdìng hǎole, shāohòu nín huì shōu dào yùdìng yóujiàn。
服务员：李先生，您的房间预订好了，稍后您会收到预订邮件。

Lǐ Wěi: Hǎo de, xièxie!
李伟：好的，谢谢！

Fúwùyuán: Bú kèqi, qǐngwèn hái yǒu shénme kěyǐ bāng nín ma?
服务员：不客气，请问还有什么可以帮您吗？

Lǐ Wěi: Méiyǒu le, xièxie!
李 伟：没有 了，谢谢！

Fúwùyuán: Xièxie nín xuǎnzé Méigui Jiǔdiàn, zhù nín shēnghuó yúkuài!
服务员：谢谢 您 选择 玫瑰 酒店，祝 您 生活 愉快！

生词 New words

1	请问	qǐngwèn	动	May I ask…?
2	帮	bāng	动	to help
3	预订	yùdìng	动	to book
4	酒店	jiǔdiàn	名	hotel
5	这里	zhèlǐ	代	here
6	房间	fángjiān	名	room
7	还是	háishi	连	…or…
8	钱	qián	名	money
9	天	tiān	名	day
10	早餐	zǎocān	名	breakfast
11	美元	měiyuán	名	dollar
12	住	zhù	动	to live

13	确认	quèrèn	动	to confirm
14	姓名	xìngmíng	名	name
15	护照	hùzhào	名	passport
16	号码	hàomǎ	名	number
17	稍后	shāohòu	副	later
18	收到	shōu dào		to receive
19	邮件	yóujiàn	名	e-mail/letter
20	祝	zhù	动	to wish
21	生活	shēnghuó	名	life
22	愉快	yúkuài	形	happy
专有名词 Proper Nouns				
23	李伟	Lǐ Wěi	名	Liwei
24	曼谷	Màngǔ	名	Bangkok
25	玫瑰 酒店	Méigui Jiǔdiàn	名	Rose Hotel

语言点　Language points

1. 请问……

Excuse me, may I ask…?

Qǐngwèn, nín de xìngmíng shì shénme?
(1) 请问，您的姓名是什么？

Qǐngwèn, nín zhù jǐ tiān?
(2) 请问，您住几天？

Qǐngwèn, nín de diànhuà hàomǎ shì duōshao?
(3) 请问，您的电话号码是多少？

2. ×月×号

Date

Jul.	18th	Nov.	2nd
↓	↓	↓	↓
7 月 (yuè)	18 号 (hào) / 日 (rì)	11 月 (yuè)	2 号 (hào) / 日 (rì)

3. ……多少钱？

How much…? / What is the price/rate for…?

Dān rén jiān duōshao qián?
(1) 单 人 间 多少 钱？

Shuāng rén jiān duōshao qián?
(2) 双 人 间 多少 钱？

Zǎocān duōshao qián?
(3) 早餐 多少 钱？

měiyuán 美元　　rénmínbì 人民币

练习 Exercises

1. 看图片说词。

Speak out the words according to the pictures.

 (1) ________	 (2) ________

（3）________________

（4）________________

（5）________________

（6）________________

2. 根据图片内容完成对话。

Complete the dialogue according to the pictures.

(1) A: ______________________?

Nínhǎo! Wǒ yào yùdìng
B: 您好! 我 要 预订

yí gè fángjiān。
一 个 房间。

(2) A: ______________________?

Wǒ yào yùdìng yuè hào de
B: 我 要 预订 4 月 15 号 的

fángjiān。
房间。

(3) A: ______________________?

Wǒde hùzhào hàomǎ shì
B: 我的 护照 号码 是

wǒ de
CN7832, 我 的 e-mail

shì
是 liwei@163. com。

房价表

ROOM RATE

单人间	¥480
双人间	¥550
三人间	¥620

Qǐngwèn shuāng rén jiān
(4) A: 请问 双 人 间

duōshao qián?
多少 钱?

B: ______________________。

3. 情景练习。

Practice speaking.

根据要求，帮助这位中国客人预订房间。

中国商人刘东和他的老板 10 月 18 号要去印尼出差两天，刘东打电话到印尼大酒店预订两个单人间，你是印尼大酒店前台服务员，请你帮助刘东预订房间。

Chinese businessman Liu Dong and his boss are going to Indonesia for a two-day business trip on October 18th. Liu Dong calls the Indonesia Hotel to book two single rooms. You are the front desk clerk of the Indonesia Hotel. Please help Liu Dong to make a reservation.

房价表

ROOM RATE

单人间	$78（有早餐）
双人间	$90（有早餐）
三人间	$118（有早餐）

LiúDōng

姓名：刘　东

号码：CN8097

邮箱：liud@sina.com

WángHuī

姓名：王　辉

号码：CN3339

小知识 Notes

网上怎么订酒店房间

（1）在网上搜索提供酒店预订服务的网站。目前在中国，较大的酒店预订网站有携程网、同程网、去哪儿网等几个网站，以下以携程网站订房过程为例。

（2）进入网站页面，注册一个账号。

（3）在预订页面：

①选择你要去的地区（国家、地区、城市）。

②选择入住和退房的时间。

③点击“搜索”，网站页面就会出现许多酒店。

④网页出现的酒店一般是按照“受欢迎程度”进行排列的，页面上还可以根据“具体位置”“价格”“支付方式”“是否有早餐”“房型”等条件进行查找，您根据自己的要求进行选择即可。

⑤选择喜欢的酒店点击“预订”，进入支付页面，填写预订信息，在线支付（中国支持微信、支付宝等多种支付方式）就完成预订了。

国外酒店预订的方式有很多，除了中国人常用的携程、飞猪、去哪儿以外，还有很多特价酒店预订网站，比如 Booking、Agoda、Hotels、Kayak 等都是国外预订酒店的热门网站。

How to Book a Hotel Room Online

(1) Search the websites that offer online hotel reservation service. At present, there are several major websites in China, such as Ctrip. com, LY. com and Qunar. com. The following is an example of the room booking process on Ctrip. com.

(2) Go to the website and register an account.

(3) On the booking page:

①Choose the place (country, region, city) you want to visit.

②Choose the time of check-in and check-out.

③Click "Search" and many hotels will appear on the website page.

④The hotels appearing on the web page are generally arranged by "popularity". You can also research by "specific location" "price" "payment method" "availability of breakfast" "room type" and other conditions according to your needs.

⑤Select the hotel you like and click "Book" to enter the payment page, fill in the reservation information, and pay online (Wechat, Alipay and some other payment methods are supported in China) to complete the reservation.

There are many ways to book hotels abroad. In addition to Ctrip, Fliggy and Qunar, which are commonly used by Chinese people, there are also many overseas hotel booking websites with special offers, such as Booking, Agoda, Hotels and Kayak, which are all popular websites for booking hotels abroad.

第二课

欢迎您入住玫瑰酒店

课前热身 Warming up

1. 你知道怎么办理酒店入住吗？

   Do you know how to check in at a hotel?

2. 入住酒店时，你一般喜欢住什么样的房间？

   When you stay in a hofel, what kind of room do you usually prefer?

课文 Text

中国商人李伟到曼谷出差，他已经预订了玫瑰酒店的房间。现在他到达了玫瑰酒店前台办理入住。

Chinese businessman Li Wei is on a business trip to Bangkok. He has booked a room at the Rose Hotel. Now he is checking in at the front desk of the hotel.

Lǐ Wěi
李 伟

中国商人

A business man from China

fúwùyuán
服务员

酒店前台

a waitress at the front desk

Fúwùyuán: Nín hǎo! Huānyíng lái dào Méigui Jiǔdiàn! Qǐngwèn yǒu shénme kěyǐ bāng nín?
服务员：您 好！ 欢迎 来 到 玫瑰 酒店！ 请问 有 什么 可以 帮 您？

Lǐ Wěi: Nín hǎo! Wǒ yùdìng le yuè hào dào hào de fángjiān。
李 伟：您 好！我 预订 了 7 月 18 号 到 21 号 的 房间。

Fúwùyuán: Hǎo de, xiānsheng。Qǐngwèn yùdìng xìngmíng shì shénme?
服务员：好 的， 先生。 请问 预订 姓名 是 什么？

Lǐ Wěi: Lǐ Wěi。
李 伟：李 伟。

Fúwùyuán: Qǐng shāo děng, wǒ chá yíxià。Lǐ xiānsheng, nín yùdìng de shì
服务员：请 稍 等，我 查 一下。李 先生， 您 预订 的 是

yuè hào dào hào de dān rén jiān, yǒu zǎocān。
7 月 18 号 到 21 号 的 单 人 间，有 早餐。

Lǐ Wěi: Duì de。
李 伟：对 的。

Fúwùyuán: Lǐ xiānsheng, qǐng gěi wǒ nín de hùzhào。
服务员：李 先生，请 给 我 您 的 护照。

Lǐ Wěi: Gěi nín。
李 伟：给 您。

Fúwùyuán: Xièxie, qǐng shāo děng!
服务员：谢谢，请 稍 等！

Lǐ Wěi: Hǎo de。
李 伟：好 的。

Fúwùyuán: Lǐ xiānsheng, nín xūyào fù měiyuán yājīn。Kěyǐ shuākā, yě kěyǐ fù xiànjīn。
服务员：李 先生，您 需要 付 80 美元 押金。可以 刷卡，也 可以 付 现金。

Lǐ Wěi: Qǐngwèn xiànjīn kěyǐ yòng rénmínbì ma?
李 伟：请问 现金 可以 用 人民币 吗？

Fúwùyuán: Bùhǎoyìsi, xiānsheng, zhǐ néng yòng měiyuán huò tàizhū。
服务员：不好意思，先生，只 能 用 美元 或 泰铢。

Lǐ Wěi: Hǎo de, wǒ shuākǎ。
李 伟：好 的，我 刷卡。

Fúwùyuán: Hǎo de, qǐng nín shūrù mìmǎ。……Qǐng zài zhèlǐ qiānmíng。
服务员：好 的，请 您 输入 密码。……请 在 这里 签名。

Zhè shì nín de yínháng shuākǎ xiǎopiào, qǐng ná hǎo。
这 是 您 的 银行 刷卡 小票，请 拿 好。

Lǐ Wěi: Xièxie, wǒ de fángjiān zài jǐ céng?
李 伟：谢谢，我 的 房间 在 几 层？

Fúwùyuán: Xiànzài yǒu céng hé céng de fángjiān, nín xiǎng zhù jǐ céng?
服务员：现在 有 10 层 和 12 层 的 房间，您 想 住 几 层？

Lǐ Wěi: céng。Wǒ xǐhuan gāocéng de fángjiān。
李　伟：12 层。我 喜欢 高层 的 房间。

Fúwùyuán: Hǎo de, qǐng shāo děng。Lǐ Wěi, Nín de fángjiān shì zhè shì nín de fángkǎ。Zǎocān shì měi tiān zǎoshang diǎn dào diǎn, zài céng cāntīng。
服务员：好 的，请 稍 等。李 伟，您 的 房间 是 1208，这 是 您 的 房卡。早餐 是 每 天 早上 6 点 到 9 点，在 1 层 餐厅。

Lǐ Wěi: Fēicháng gǎnxiè!
李　伟：非常 感谢！

Fúwùyuán: Huānyíng rùzhù Méigui Jiǔdiàn, zhù nín shēnghuó yúkuài!
服务员：欢迎 入住 玫瑰 酒店，祝 您 生活 愉快！

生词 New words

1	欢迎	huānyíng	动	to welcome
2	入住	rùzhù	动	to check in
3	需要	xūyào	动	to need
4	喜欢	xǐhuan	动	to like
5	稍等	shāo děng		to wait for a while
6	查	chá	动	to search
7	给	gěi	动	to give

8	付	fù	动	to pay
9	押金	yājīn	名	deposit
10	刷卡	shuākǎ	动	to pay by card
11	现金	xiànjīn	名	cash
12	只能	zhǐ néng		only can
13	用	yòng	动	to use
14	输入	shūrù	动	to enter，to input
15	密码	mìmǎ	名	password
16	签名	qiānmíng	动	to sign
17	小票	xiǎopiào	名	receipt
18	拿	ná	动	to take
19	层	céng	量	floor
20	高	gāo	形	high
21	房卡	fángkǎ	名	room/key card
22	餐厅	cāntīng	名	restaurant
23	非常	fēicháng	副	very much
24	感谢	gǎnxiè	动	thank

语言点 Language points

1. 请稍等/请等一下。

Please wait for a moment.

Nín hǎo! Qǐngwèn wǒ de fángjiān zài jǐ céng?
(1) A：您 好！请问 我 的 房间 在 几 层？

Qǐng shāo děng, wǒ chá yíxià。
B：请 稍 等，我 查 一下。

Nín hǎo! Wǒ zhǎo Lǐ lǎoshī。
(2) A：您 好！我 找 李 老师。

Qǐng děng yíxià, wǒ qù jiào tā。
B：请 等 一下，我 去 叫 他。

2. 可以刷卡，也可以付现金。

Either credit card or cash will do.

shuākǎ
(1) 刷卡 pay by card

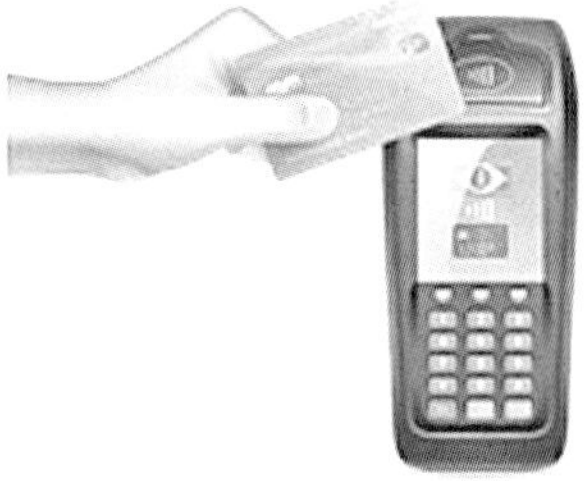

yínhángkǎ xìnyòngkǎ
银行卡 / 信用卡

Bank Card/Credit Card

shuākǎ xiǎopiào
刷卡 小票

bank receipt

fù xiànjīn
(2) 付 现金 pay in cash

shǒujī fù qián
(3) 手机 付 钱 mobile payment

WeChat Pay

wēixìn zhīfù
微信 支付Wechat pay

支 Alipay™

zhīfù bǎo zhīfù
支付 宝 支付Alipay

kěyǐ yě kěyǐ
(4) 可以……, 也 可以…… either..., or...

Nín kěyǐ zhù céng, yě kěyǐ zhù céng。
①您 可以 住 10 层, 也 可以 住 12 层。

Nín kěyǐ zhù dān rén jiān, yě kěyǐ zhù shuāng rén jiān。
②您 可以 住 单 人 间, 也 可以 住 双 人 间。

3. 不好意思，……

Sorry，…

　　　Bùhǎoyìsi，zhǐ néng yòng měiyuán。
(1) 不好意思，只 能 用 美元。

　　　Bùhǎoyìsi，zhǐyǒu shuāng rén jiān。
(2) 不好意思，只有 双 人 间。

　　　Bùhǎoyìsi，　měiyuán de dān rén jiān méiyǒu zǎocān。
(3) 不好意思，60 美元 的 单 人 间 没有 早餐。

练习　Exercises

1. 看图片说词。

Speak out the words according to the pictures.

(1) ____________

(2) ____________

 (3) ________	 (4) ________
 (5) ________	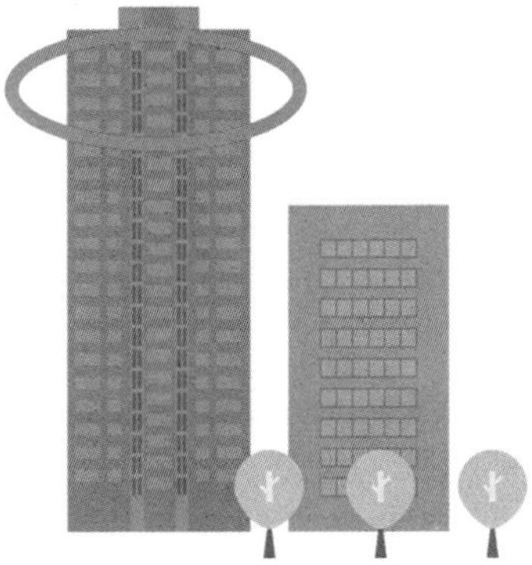 (6) ________

2. 短语连线，并完成句子。

Match the phrases and complete the sentences.

护照	预订	入住	付	输入	请
密码	稍等	号码	酒店	现金	房间

Nín hǎo, wǒ yào
(1) 您 好，我 要 ________________。

Qǐngwèn, nín de shì duōshao?
(2) 请问，您 的 ________________是 多少？

wǒ chá yíxià.
(3) ________________，我 查 一下。

Huānyíng nín Zhù nín shēnghuó yúkuài!
(4) 欢迎 您________________！祝 您 生活 愉快！

Qǐng zài zhèlǐ qiānmíng.
(5) 请 ________________，在 这里 签名。

Nín kěyǐ shuākǎ, yě kěyǐ
(6) 您 可以 刷卡，也 可以 ________________。

3. 情景练习。

Practice speaking.

根据要求，帮助这位中国客人办理入住。

中国商人刘东和他的老板今天（10 月 18 日）到达印尼大酒店，他们要在酒店住两天，他们已经预订了房间。刘东的老板喜欢住在高层的房间。你是印尼大酒店前台服务员，请你帮助他们办理入住。

Chinese businessman Liu Dong and his boss arrived at the Indonesia Hotel today (October 18th). They will stay in the hotel for two days. They have already booked rooms. Liu Dong's boss likes to stay in a room on an upper floor. You are the front desk clerk of the Indonesia Hotel. Please help them check in.

小知识 Notes

中国人选择酒店房间的小心思

1. 不喜欢电梯旁边的房间

因为电梯旁边的房间，一般来往的人很多，比较吵闹，尤其是睡眠困难的人，最不喜欢电梯旁边的房间。

2. 不喜欢走廊最里面的房间

第一，走廊最里面的位置离安全逃生口或电梯都比较远，如果发生火灾等其他安全事故时，逃生困难，危险高。第二，走廊里的监控常常拍摄不到位，如果发生突发事件，想要调取监控也是比较困难。第三，除了安全问题，还有清洁问题，走廊尽头的房间常常是卫生死角。因此大部分人不喜欢这样的房间。

3. 不喜欢选择镜子对着床的房间

有一些酒店，为了让房间里的空间更加开阔，喜欢在房间里设计各种玻璃推拉门窗，比如对着床是透明的玻璃，有些卫生间也都是玻璃拉门，晚上睡觉，感觉随时能看到自己，这样的设置很没有安全感，一不小心，真会把人给吓醒。所以大部分人喜欢的房间是打开门是房间的走廊，床的一边是贴着卫生间的墙。

（本文选自“知乎”，作者：英子同学：《住酒店该怎么挑选比较好的房间》，有改动）

Chinese People Choose Their Hotel Rooms Carefully

1. **They don't like the room next to the elevator**

Generally, there are many people coming and going near the door of the room next to the elevator, so it is noisy. Especially for people who have difficulty sleeping, the room next to the elevator is their least favorite room.

2. **They don't like the room at the end of the hallway**

Firstly, the innermost position of the corridor is far away from the emergency exit or elevator. In case of fire and other safety accidents, escape is difficult and the risk is high. Secondly, the surveillance here is often not in place. If an emergency occurs, it is difficult to retrieve the surveillance video. Thirdly, in addition to safety issues, there are hygiene issues. The room at the end of the corridor is often a sanitary dead zone. Therefore, most people don't like such rooms.

3. **They don't like to choose a room with a mirror facing the bed**

In order to make the room look more spacious, some hotels like to design all kinds of glass sliding doors and windows, some are facing the bed. Sleeping at night, people seem to feel that they can see themselves at any time. The setting can be so insecure that people may feel frightened and wake up.

Therefore, most people prefer a room with the door opening into the hallway and one side of the bed against the bathroom wall.

第三课

您好，请填一下行李寄存单

课前热身 Warming up

1. 你知道怎么办理行李寄存吗？

   Do you know how to store your luggage?

2. 酒店支付房费的方式有哪些？

   What are the ways to pay for the hotel rooms?

课文 Text

中国商人李伟在曼谷出差已经结束了，今天要离开玫瑰酒店，他去到前台办理退房，并且打算寄存行李。

Chinese businessman Li Wei has finished his business trip in Bangkok. He is leaving Rose Hotel today. He is going to check out at the front desk and plan to store his luggage.

Lǐ Wěi
李 伟

中国商人

A business man from China

fúwùyuán
服务员

酒店前台

a waitress at the front desk

Fúwùyuán：Nín hǎo！Qǐngwèn yǒu shénme kěyǐ bāng nín？
服务员：您 好！ 请问 有 什么 可以 帮 您？

Lǐ Wěi：Nín hǎo！Wǒ yào bànlǐ tuì fáng。
李 伟：您 好！我 要 办理 退 房。

Fúwùyuán：Hǎo de，Qǐngwèn nín de fángjiān hàomǎ shì duōshao？
服务员：好 的，请问 您 的 房间 号码 是 多少？

Lǐ Wěi：Zhè shì wǒ de fángkǎ。
李 伟：1208。这 是 我 的 房卡。

Fúwùyuán：Xièxie！qǐng shāo děng，wǒ chá yíxià。
服务员：谢谢！请 稍 等，我 查 一下。

Lǐ Wěi: Hǎo de。
李 伟：好 的。

Fúwùyuán: Lǐ xiānsheng, nín yuè hào rùzhù, hào tuì fáng, nín zhù le sān tiān, qǐng nín quèrèn yí xià。
服务员：李 先生， 您 7 月 18 号 入住，21 号 退 房， 您 住 了 三 天， 请 您 确认 一下。

Lǐ Wěi: Duì de。
李 伟：对 的。

Fúwùyuán: Fángfèi shì měiyuán yìtiān, yígòng shì měiyuán。Qǐngwèn nín shuākǎ háishi fù xiànjīn?
服务员：房费 是 88 美元 一天， 一共 是 264 美元。 请问 您 刷卡 还是 付 现金？

Lǐ Wěi: Shuākǎ。
李 伟：刷卡。

Fúwùyuán: Qǐng shūrù mìmǎ。…… Qǐng zài zhèlǐ qiānmíng。Nín de yínháng kǎ hé xiǎopiào, qǐng nín ná hǎo!
服务员：请 输入 密码。…… 请 在 这里 签名。 您 的 银行 卡 和 小票， 请 您 拿 好！

Lǐ Wěi: Wǒ xūyào fángfèi shōujù hé zhùsù dān, kěyǐ dǎyìn gěi wǒ ma?
李 伟：我 需要 房费 收据 和 住宿 单，可以 打印 给 我 吗？

Fúwùyuán: Hǎo de, qǐng shāo děng! Zhè shì shōujù hé zhùsù dān。
服务员：好 的，请 稍 等！ 这 是 收据 和 住宿 单。

Lǐ Wěi: Qǐngwèn, zhèlǐ kěyǐ jìcún xíngli ma? Wǒ yào chūqù yí xià, dài xíngli bù fāngbiàn。
李 伟： 请问， 这里 可以 寄存 行李 吗？我 要 出去 一下，带 行李 不 方便。

Fúwùyuán: Kěyǐ de, qǐng nín tián yíxià xíngli jìcún dān。
服务员：可以 的，请 您 填 一下 行李 寄存 单。

Lǐ Wěi: Tián hǎole, zhè shì wǒ de xíngli xiāng。
李 伟：填 好了，这 是 我 的 行李 箱。

Fúwùyuán: Nín huílái yǐhòu, píng xíngli dān jiù kěyǐ ná xíngli。
服务员：您 回来 以后，凭 行李 单 就 可以 拿 行李。

Lǐ Wěi：Xièxie！
李　伟：谢谢！

Fúwùyuán：Bú kèqi，xūyào gěi nín jiào yí liàng chūzūchē ma？
服务员：不客气，需要给您叫一辆出租车吗？

Lǐ Wěi：Hǎo de。
李　伟：好的。

Fúwùyuán：Qǐng nín zài ménkǒu shāo děng，chūzūchē yíhuìr jiù lái。Zhù nín chūxíng yúkuài！
服务员：请您在门口稍等，出租车一会儿就来。祝您出行愉快！

Lǐ Wěi：Xièxie！
李　伟：谢谢！

生词　New words

1	填	tián	动	to fill in（form，sheet）
2	行李	xíngli	名	luggage
3	寄存	jìcún	动	to deposit
4	单	dān	名	sheet
5	办理	bànlǐ	动	to handle
6	退房	tuì fáng		to check out

7	房费	fángfèi	名	room rate
8	一共	yígòng	副	in total
9	收据	shōujù	名	receipt
10	住宿	zhùsù	动	get accommodation
11	打印	dǎyìn	动	to print
12	带	dài	动	to take with
13	箱	xiāng	名	suitcase
14	凭	píng	介	depend on
15	辆	liàng	量	vehicle (a measure word)
16	出租车	chūzūchē	名	taxi
17	门口	ménkǒu	名	doorway
18	出行	chūxíng	动	to go for a trip

语言点 Language points

1. 凭……就可以……
depend on/based on...

Nín píng fángkǎ jiù kěyǐ chī zǎocān。
(1) 您 凭 房卡 就 可以 吃 早餐。

Nín píng yājīn xiǎopiào jiù kěyǐ tuì yājīn。
(2) 您 凭 押金 小票 就 可以 退 押金。

Nín píng xíngli dān jiù kěyǐ ná xíngli。
(3) 您 凭 行李 单 就 可以 拿 行李。

2. 叫一辆出租车
call a taxi

叫：call (a taxi/food delivery service) ... for someone

叫出租车/叫外卖

Wǒ bāng nín jiào yí liàng chūzūchē。
(1) 我 帮 您 叫 一 辆 出租车。

Wǒ bāng nǐ jiào yí fèn wàimài。
(2) 我 帮 你 叫 一 份 外卖。

练习 Exercises

1. 看图片说词。

Speak out the words according to the pictures.

(1) ________________

(2) ________________

(3) ________________

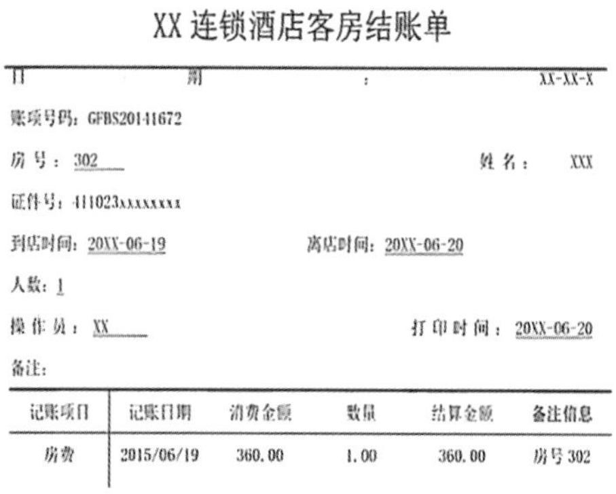

XX 连锁酒店客房结账单

日期：XX-XX-X

账项号码：GFBS20141672

房号：302　　姓名：XXX

证件号：411023xxxxxxxx

到店时间：20XX-06-19　　离店时间：20XX-06-20

人数：1

操作员：XX　　打印时间：20XX-06-20

备注：

记账项目	记账日期	消费金额	数量	结算金额	备注信息
房费	2015/06/19	360.00	1.00	360.00	房号 302

(4) ________________

(5) ______________

(6) ______________

2. 短语连线，并完成句子。

Match the phrases and complete the sentences.

办理	房间	打印	付	寄存	一辆
收据	行李	号码	退房	出租车	房费

Nín hǎo, zhè shì wǒ de fángkǎ, wǒ yào
(1) 您 好，这 是 我 的 房卡，我 要 ______________。

Qǐngwèn, nín de ______________ shì duōshao?
(2) 请问，您 的 ______________ 是 多少？

Qǐngwèn, zhèlǐ kěyǐ ______________ ma? Wǒ de xíngli tài duō le。
(3) 请问，这里 可以 ______________ 吗？我 的 行李 太 多 了。

Qǐngwèn nín zěnme ______________? Shuākǎ háishi fù xiànjīn?
(4) 请问 您 怎么 ______________？刷卡 还是 付 现金？

Qǐng gěi wǒ ______ hé zhùsù dān, xièxie!

(5) 请 给 我 ______ 和 住宿 单，谢谢！

Xūyào gěi nín jiào ______ ma?

(6) 需要 给 您 叫 ______ 吗？

3. 根据图片内容完成对话。

Complete the dialogue according to the pictures.

(1) A: ______?

Wǒ de fángjiān shì

B: 我 的 房间 是 1206。

(2) A: ______?

Wǒ shuākǎ.

B: 我 刷卡。

Qǐngwèn, kěyǐ jìcún xíngli ma?

(3) A: 请问，可以 寄存 行李 吗？

B: ______。

(4) A: ______?

Hǎo de, xièxie!

B: 好 的，谢谢！

4. 情景练习。

Practice speaking.

根据要求，帮助这位中国客人办理退房。

中国商人刘东和他的老板今天（10 月 2 日）要离开印尼，他们吃完午饭以后要办理退房，退房以后他们打算先去附近逛逛，需要先把行李寄存在前台。你是印尼大酒店前台服务员，请你帮助他们退房和办理行李寄存。

Chinese businessman Liu Dong and his boss will leave Indonesia today (October 2nd). They will check out after lunch. After checking out, they plan to go around and do some shopping, so they need to deposit their luggage at the front desk. You are the front desk clerk of the Indonesia Hotel. Please help them check out and deposit luggage.

小知识 Notes

酒店行李寄存知多少

（1）酒店一般会免费为住店客人提供行李寄存服务，寄存行李时请出示房卡，行李寄存期限根据各酒店要求，一般是三天到一个月不等，超过时限将收取寄存费用。

（2）禁止存放枪支弹药、易燃易爆危险物品、毒品等违法物品以及腐蚀放射性等物品。

（3）寄存易碎物品时，应事先告知酒店，如果发生损坏或污染他人物品，由寄存客人承担损失及相关赔偿。

（4）机密文件、保密图纸等重要资料，各种现金、有价票证、金银首饰和电子类产品等贵重物品不予寄存。

（5）寄存食品类物品时，如产生腐烂、异味或过期，酒店将不负责。因此像水果、蛋糕、点心等食物寄存时间不宜过长。

（6）酒店对客人寄存行李有保管责任，客人应凭行李寄存单领取行李，由酒店工作人员核对无误后方可取走。

（7）如果因酒店员工疏忽而造成行李丢失的，酒店将对客人进行赔偿。

How Much do You Know about Hotel Luggage Storage

(1) The hotel generally provides free luggage storage service for guests. Please show your room card when you deposit your luggage. The luggage storage period varies from 3 days to 1 month according to the requirements of each hotel. The storage fee will be charged if the time limit is exceeded.

(2) It is prohibited to store guns and ammunition, inflammable and explosive dangerous items, drugs and other illegal items, as well as corrosive radioactive items.

(3) The hotel shall be informed in advance when fragile items are stored. In case of damage or contamination of other people's belongings, the depositor shall bear liability for the loss and related compensation.

(4) Confidential documents, confidential drawings and other important materials, all kinds of cash, valuable tickets, gold and silver jewelry, electronic

products and other valuable items shall not be deposited.

(5) The hotel will not be responsible for food items that are rotten, smelly or expired. Therefore, food such as fruits, cakes and snacks should not be stored for too long.

(6) The hotel is responsible for the safe custody of the luggage stored by the guests. Guests shall claim the luggage with the luggage deposit slip. The guests can only take the luggage away after being checked by the hotel staff.

(7) If the baggage is lost due to the negligence of the hotel staff, the hotel shall compensate the guests.

第四课

您好，请问您需要订餐吗

课前热身 Warming up

1. 你知道怎么预订房间送餐服务吗？

   Do you know how to book room service?

2. 你国家的美食代表菜有哪些？

   What are the typical dishes of your country?

课文 Text

李伟入住酒店以后，觉得有点儿累，不想出去吃晚饭，他想叫客房送餐服务。他打电话到餐饮部订餐。

After Li Wei checked into the hotel, he felt a little tired and didn't want to go out for dinner. He wanted to order room service. He called the catering department to order food.

Lǐ Wěi
李 伟

中国商人

A business man from China

fúwùyuán
服务员

餐饮部服务员

a waitress of catering department

Lǐ　Wěi：Nín hǎo！Qǐngwèn shì cānyǐng bù ma？
李　伟：您 好！ 请问 是 餐饮 部 吗？

Fúwùyuán：Nín hǎo！ Zhelǐ shì cānyǐng bù。Qǐngwèn nín xūyào dìngcān ma？
服务员：您 好！这里 是 餐饮 部。 请问 您 需要 订餐 吗？

Lǐ　Wěi：Shì de，wǒ yào yùdìng wǎncān。
李　伟：是 的，我 要 预订 晚餐。

Fúwùyuán：Nín yào sòng cān háishi dào cāntīng chī ne？
服务员：您 要 送 餐 还是 到 餐厅 吃 呢？

Lǐ　Wěi：Wǒ yào sòng cān。
李　伟：我 要 送 餐。

Fúwùyuán: Hǎo de。Wǎncān càidān fàng zài chájī shang, nín kěyǐ kàn kan。
服务员：好 的。晚餐 菜单 放 在 茶几 上，您 可以 看 看。

Lǐ Wěi: Qǐngwèn yǒu shénme tuījiàn ma?
李 伟：请问 有 什么 推荐 吗?

Fúwùyuán: Jīntiān wǎncān de zhǔshí shì miànshí, niúnǎn miàn de wèidào fēicháng búcuò, nín kěyǐ shì shi。
服务员：今天 晚餐 的 主食 是 面食，牛腩 面 的 味道 非常 不错，您 可以 试 试。

Lǐ Wěi: Yào yì wǎn niúnǎn miàn。
李 伟：要 一 碗 牛腩 面。

Fúwùyuán: Hǎo de, hái yào bié de ma?
服务员：好 的，还 要 别 的 吗?

Lǐ Wěi: Zài yào yí gè jī ròu hàn bǎo, yì bēi sūdá shuǐ。
李 伟：再 要 一 个 鸡 肉 汉 堡，一 杯 苏打 水。

Fúwùyuán: Hǎo de, qǐngwèn sūdá shuǐ jiā bīng ma?
服务员：好 的，请问 苏打 水 加 冰 吗?

Lǐ Wěi: Bù jiā bīng, xièxie!
李 伟：不 加 冰，谢谢!

Fúwùyuán: Hǎo de。Nín yào yì wǎn niúnǎn miàn, yí gè jī ròu hàn bǎo hé yì bēi sūdá shuǐ, bù jiā bīng, qǐng nín quèrèn yíxià。
服务员：好 的。您 要 一 碗 牛腩 面，一 个 鸡 肉 汉 堡 和 一 杯 苏打 水，不 加 冰，请 您 确认 一下。

Lǐ Wěi: Duì de。
李 伟：对 的。

Fúwùyuán: Hǎo de, xiānsheng。Wǎncān huì zài xàiwǔ diǎn dào diǎnbàn zhījiān sòng dào nín de fángjiān。Qǐngwèn nín de fángjiān hàomǎ shì duōshao?
服务员：好 的，先生。晚餐 会 在 下午 6 点 到 6 点 半 之间 送 到 您 的 房间。请问 您 的 房间 号码 是 多少?

Lǐ Wěi:
李 伟：1208。

Fúwùyuán：Hǎo de，nín de wǎncān yǐjīng yùdìng chénggōng，cān fèi huì jì
服务员：好 的，您 的 晚餐 已经 预定 成功，餐 费 会 记

zài nín de fángfèi shang。Nín tuì fáng shí，yìqǐ jiésuàn。
在 您 的 房费 上。您 退 房 时，一起 结算。

Lǐ Wěi：Hǎo de，xièxie！
李 伟：好 的，谢谢！

生词 New words

1	订餐	dìng cān		to order dinner
2	送餐	sòng cān		food delivery
3	餐饮部	cānyǐn bù		the Food and Beverage Department
4	晚餐	wǎncān	名	dinner
5	菜单	càidān	名	menu
6	茶几	chájī	名	tea table
7	推荐	tuījiàn	动	to recommend
8	主食	zhǔshí	名	main food
9	牛腩面	niúnǎn miàn		sirloin noodles
10	味道	wèidào	名	taste

11	碗	wǎn	量	bowl
12	再	zài	副	again
13	汉堡	hàn bǎo		hamburger
14	杯	bēi	量	cup
15	苏打水	sūdá shuǐ		soda water
16	加冰	jiā bīng		to put with ice
17	之间	zhī jiān		between
18	结算	jiésuàn	动	to settle accounts

语言点 Language points

1. "您可以试试。/您可以看看。"

You can give sth. a try/have a try.

You can have a look.

Jī ròu hàn bǎo hěn hǎo chī, nín kěyǐ shì shi。
(1) 鸡肉汉堡很好吃，您可以试试。

Shuāng rén jiān hěn dà, nín kěyǐ kàn kan。
(2) 双人间很大，您可以看看。

Píngguǒ zhī wèidào búcuò, nín kěyǐ cháng chang。
(3) 苹果汁（apple juice）味道不错，您可以尝尝。

2. “一碗牛腩面、一个鸡肉汉堡、一杯苏打水。”

A bowl of beef brisket noodle, a chicken hamburger, a bottle of soda.

wǎn 碗 bowl  yì wǎn miàn 一 碗 面	gè 个  yí gè hàn bǎo 一 个 汉 堡	bēi 杯 cup  yì bēi shuǐ 一 杯 水

fèn 份  yí fèn niúpái 一 份 牛排	píng 瓶 bottle 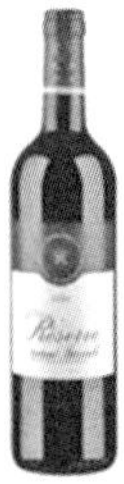 yì píng jiǔ 一 瓶 酒

3. 时间的表达。

Describe Times.

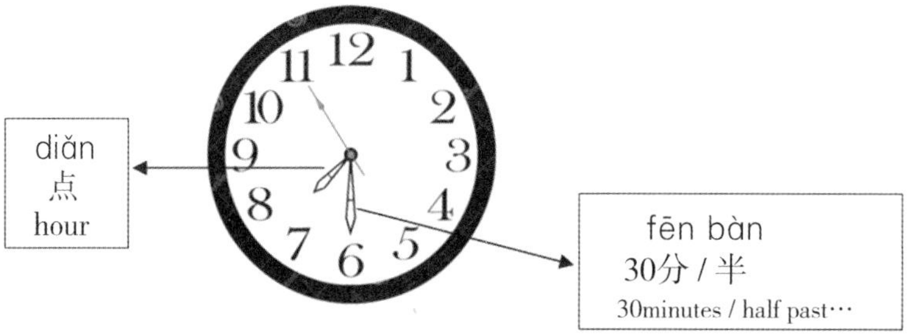

7：30 ⇨ 7点30分/7点半

练习 Exercises

1. 看图片说词。

Speak out the words according to the pictures.

 (1) ________	 (2) ________

 （3）________	 （4）________
 （5）________	 （6）________

2. 短语连线，并完成句子。

Match the phrases and complete the sentences.

预订	看看	一碗	一个	6点	一杯
汉堡	水	菜单	晚餐	牛腩面	送餐

Nín hǎo, zhèlǐ shì cānyǐn bù。Qǐngwèn nín yào ______ ma?
(1) 您好，这里是餐饮部。请问您要______吗？

Wǒ yào ______, bù jiā bīng。
(2) 我要______，不加冰。

Wǒ xǐhuan chī miànshí, qǐng gěi wǒ ______。
(3) 我喜欢吃面食，请给我______。

Wǒ zài yào ______, yígòng duōshao qián?
(4) 我再要______，一共多少钱？

Nín kěyǐ ______, jīntiān de zhǔshí shì miànshí。
(5) 您可以______，今天的主食是面食。

Qǐngwèn, ______ kěyǐ ma?
(6) 请问，______可以吗？

3. 根据图片内容完成对话。

Complete the dialogue according to the pictures.

(1) A: ______?

Nín hǎo wǒ yào dìng wǎncān。
B: 您好！我要订晚餐。

Qǐngwèn yǒu shénme tuījiàn ma?
(2) A: 请问有什么推荐吗？

B: ______。

qǐng nín
（3）A：________，请 您

quèrèn yíxià。
确认 一下。

Duì de。
B：对 的。

Qǐngwèn jǐ diǎn sòng cān
（4）A：请问 几 点 送 餐？

B：________________。

4. 情景练习。

Practice speaking.

根据要求，帮助这位中国客人预订晚餐。

刘东和他的老板见完客户回到酒店，他们有点儿累，打算在房间吃晚餐。

你是印尼大酒店餐饮部服务员，请你帮助他们订餐和送餐。

Liu Dong and his boss went back to the hotel after meeting the clients. They felt a little tired and planned to have dinner in the room. You are a waiter in the food and beverage department of the Indonesia Hotel. Please help them order and deliver food.

小知识 Notes

中外饮食文化差异知多少

1. 饮食观念的差异

中国饮食多以热食和熟食为主，比较注重食物的搭配，并且讲究“色、香、味”俱全。而西方饮食以生食、冷食、甜食、肉食为主，追求方便快捷。

2. 用餐工具的差异

中国人用餐使用的是筷子、汤匙，吃饭用碗盛。西方人则用盘子盛食物，餐具多样，刀、叉、勺等根据上菜的顺序依次排列在盘子的两边，不同的食物使用不同的餐具。

3. 就餐方式的差异

中国的宴席上，大家喜欢围餐，坐在一起，讲究热闹的气氛，这符合中国人“团圆、包容”的文化内涵。西方饮食宴席目的在于交际，因此多实行分餐制，以自助餐为流行，大家各取所需，不一定要固定在位子上，可以自由走动。

4. 餐桌就座礼仪的差异

中餐的宴请活动中，以圆桌为主。桌上的席位以来宾的身份高低进行排位。西方的宴请活动中，多用长桌，在正式宴会上，席位以距离主桌的位置远近来判断来宾身份的高低。

5. **上菜顺序的差异**

中餐上菜顺序是先上凉菜、饮料和酒，然后上热菜，再上主食，最后上甜食和水果。西餐上菜顺序通常是面包黄油、凉菜、汤、海鲜、主菜、甜点、咖啡以及水果。

（本文选自职场指南网：《中西方饮食文化差异有哪些》，有改动）

How Much do You Know about the Differences between Chinese and Foreign Food Cultures

1. **Differences in dietary concepts**

Chinese diet mainly focuses on hot food and cooked food, pay more attention to the combination of food and the "color, aroma and taste" of food. While the western diet is mainly based on raw food, cold food, sweet food and meat, pursuing convenience.

2. **Differences in dining tools**

Chinese people use chopsticks, spoons and bowls for meals. Westerners use plates to serve food with various tableware. Knives, forks and spoons are arranged on both sides of the plate according to the order of serving, and different tableware is used for different food.

3. **Differences in dining styles**

In Chinese banquets, people like to sit around the table and enjoy the lively atmosphere, which is in line with the Chinese culture of "reunion and inclusiveness". The purpose of western banquet is to communicate, so the serving of individual dishes is often implemented. Buffets are popular. Everybody takes what they need. They don't have to sit in a fixed seat and they can move around freely.

4. Differences in seating etiquette

Chinese banquets are dominated by round tables. The seats at the table are arranged according to the status of the guests. In western banquets, long tables are often used. At formal banquets, the guests' status is judged by the proximity of their seats to the main table.

5. Differences in serving order

Chinese food is served in the order of cold dishes, drinks and wine first, followed by hot dishes, then staple food, and finally sweet food and fruits. Western food is usually served in the order of bread and butter, cold dishes, soup, seafood, main course, desserts, coffee and fruits.

第五课

您好，请问您订位了吗

课前热身 Warming up

1. 你知道怎么在酒店餐厅点单吗？

   Do you know how to order at the hotel restaurant?

2. 你喜欢吃几分熟的牛排？

   How do you like your steak cooked?

课文 Text

李伟今天约了一位朋友在酒店见面，他要请朋友在酒店的餐厅吃饭。下午6点，他来到餐厅，准备和朋友一起吃晚餐。

Li Wei is going to invite a friend for dinner in the hotel restaurant. At 6 p. m. , he comes to the restaurant, waiting to have dinner with his friend.

Lǐ Wěi
李 伟

中国商人

A business man from China

fúwùyuán
服务员

餐厅服务员

a waitress of the restaurant

Fúwùyuán: Nín hǎo! Huānyíng guānglín! Qǐngwèn nín dìngwèi le ma?
服务员：您好，欢迎光临！请问您订位了吗？

Lǐ Wěi: Méiyǒu, xiànzài yǒu wèizi ma?
李伟：没有，现在有位子吗？

Fúwùyuán: Yǒu de。Xiānsheng, qǐngwèn nín jǐ wèi?
服务员：有的。先生，请问您几位？

Lǐ Wěi: Liǎng wèi。Yǒu kào chuāng de wèizi ma?
李伟：两位。有靠窗的位子吗？

Fúwùyuán: Yǒu de。Xiānsheng, qǐng gēn wǒ lái。…… Zuò zhèlǐ kěyǐ ma?
服务员：有的。先生，请跟我来。……坐这里可以吗？

Lǐ Wěi: Kěyǐ。
李 伟：可以。

Fúwùyuán: Nín qǐng zuò! Zhè shì càidān, nín kěyǐ kàn kan。
服务员：您 请 坐！这 是 菜单，您 可以 看 看。

Lǐ Wěi: Hǎo de, xièxie。
李 伟：好 的，谢谢！

Fúwùyuán: Xiānsheng, jīntiān de wǎncān fēicháng fēngfù, Nín xiǎng chī diǎnr shénme ne?
服务员：先生，今天 的 晚餐 非常 丰富，您 想 吃 点儿 什么 呢？

Lǐ Wěi: Yǒu shénme tuījiàn ma?
李 伟：有 什么 推荐 吗？

Fúwùyuán: Jīntiān de niúpái fēicháng xīnxiān, nín kěyǐ shì shi。
服务员：今天 的 牛排 非常 新鲜，您 可以 试 试。

Lǐ Wěi: Yào liǎng fèn niúpái。
李 伟：要 两 份 牛排。

Fúwùyuán: Nínpái nín yào jǐ chéng shú?
服务员：牛排 您 要 几 成 熟？

Lǐ Wěi: Yí fèn qī chéng shú, yí fèn quán shú。
李 伟：一 份 七 成 熟，一 份 全 熟。

Fúwùyuán: Hǎo de, hái yào bié de ma?
服务员：好 的，还 要 别 的 吗？

Lǐ Wěi: Zài yào yí fèn shālā, yí fèn sānmíngzhì, liǎng wǎn nánguā tāng。
李 伟：再 要 一 份 沙拉，一 份 三明治，两 碗 南瓜 汤。

Fúwùyuán: Hǎo de, yǐnliào huòzhě jiǔ xūyào ma?
服务员：好 的，饮料 或者 酒 需要 吗？

Lǐ Wěi: Liǎng bēi píjiǔ, jiā bīng。
李 伟：两 杯 啤酒，加 冰。

Fúwùyuán: Hǎo de, xiānsheng, nín diǎn le liǎng fèn niúpái, yí fèn qī chéng shú、yí fèn quán shú, yí fèn shālā, yí fèn sānmíngzhì, hái yǒu
服务员：好 的，先生，您 点 了 两 份 牛排，一 份 七 成 熟、一 份 全 熟，一 份 沙拉，一 份 三明治，还 有

liǎng wǎn nánguā tāng, liǎng bēi píjiǔ, jiā bīng, duì ma?
两 碗 南瓜 汤，两 杯 啤酒，加 冰，对 吗？

Lǐ Wěi: Méi cuò, jiùshì zhèxiē。
李 伟：没 错，就是 这些。

Fúwùyuán: Hǎo de, qǐng nín shāo děng yíhuìr。Nín de cān mǎshàng
服务员：好 的，请 您 稍 等 一会儿。您 的 餐 马上

sòng lái。
送 来。

Lǐ Wěi: Hǎo de, xièxie!
李 伟：好 的，谢谢！

生词 New words

1	订位	dìngwèi	动	to book a table in a restaurant
2	吃	chī	动	to eat
3	熟	shú	形	cooked
4	位子	wèizi	名	seat
5	靠窗	kào chuāng		to sit by the window
6	跟	gēn	动	to go with
7	坐	zuò	动	to sit
8	丰富	fēngfù	形	plentiful

9	新鲜	xīnxiān	形	fresh
10	份	fèn	量	portion (a measure word)
11	沙拉	shālā	名	salad
12	三明治	sānmíngzhì	名	sandwich
13	汤	tāng	名	soup
14	饮料	yǐnliào	名	drink
15	或者	huòzhě	连	or
16	啤酒	píjiǔ	名	beer
17	点	diǎn	动	to order
18	马上	mǎshàng	副	immediately

语言点 Language points

1. “请问，您几位？”

How many in your party?

几位：How many in your party?

位：classifier for people (honorific)

Nín hǎo, qǐngwèn nín jǐ wèi?
A：您 好， 请问 您 几 位？

Liǎng wèi
B：两 位。

2. "牛排您要几成熟？"

How would like your steak cooked?

[Numbers + 成熟]

- sān chéng shú
  三 成 熟 rare
- wǔ chéng shú
  五 成 熟 medium
- qī chéng shú
  七 成 熟 medium well
- quán shú
  全 熟 well done

练习 Exercises

1. 看图片说词。

Speak out the words according to the pictures.

 (1) ______	 (2) ______
 (3) ______	 (4) ______

 (5) ________	 (6) ________

2. 读下面的句子，并根据课文内容判断对错。

Read the following sentences and mark true ("√") or false ("×").

Lǐ Wěi hé péngyou qù jiǔdiàn cāntīng chī wǎncān。
(1) 李伟和朋友去酒店餐厅吃晚餐。( )

Lǐ Wěi yùdìng le wèizi。
(2) 李伟预订了位子。( )

Lǐ Wěi yào zuò kào chuāng de wèizi。
(3) 李伟要坐靠窗的位子。( )

Jīntiān de wǎncān fēicháng fēngfù, niúpái fēicháng xīnxiān。
(4) 今天的晚餐非常丰富，牛排非常新鲜。( )

Lǐ wěi diǎn le liǎng fèn niúpái, yí fèn sān chéng shú yí fèn qī chéng shú
(5) 李伟点了两份牛排，一份三成熟，一份七成熟。( )

Lǐ Wěi hái yào shālā hé niúnǎn miàn。
(6) 李伟还要沙拉和牛腩面。( )

Wǎncān dàgài fēn zhōng zuǒyòu sòng lái。
(7) 晚餐 大概 20 分 钟 左右 送 来。( )

3. 情景练习。
Practice speaking.

根据要求，为中国客人进行晚餐服务。

刘东和老板要请两位客户在酒店的餐厅吃饭，他们想要坐在靠窗的位子，他们很喜欢吃西餐，他们还想喝酒。你是餐厅的服务员，请你为他们提供用餐服务。

Liu Dong and his boss are going to invite two clients to dinner at the hotel restaurant. They want to sit by the window. They like western food very much. They also want to drink some wine. You are a waiter in the restaurant. Please provide meal service for them.

小知识 Notes

中国餐桌礼仪的小贴士

1. 入座

座位一般是“以左为尊”。中国人宴请时，一般是使用圆桌，正对大门的位置为主座；主座左右的位置，越靠近主座地位越高；相同距离则左侧尊于右侧。

2. 上菜

一餐中式大餐，通常先上冷菜（凉拌菜、小菜等），然后是热炒，接下来是主菜，最后上点心和汤，现在受西餐的影响，很多时候会在餐后加上甜品和水果。

3. 用餐

先请客人或长辈动筷。吃饭、喝汤时声音要小，不要打扰到同桌人。有的人吃饭喜欢发出咀嚼的声音，这是很不礼貌的。夹菜时只夹面前的，不要整盘菜挑来翻去的，这样也是十分不礼貌的。

4. 倒茶和倒酒

中国人喜欢喝茶，所以中国宴席上一般有茶。当你为别人倒茶倒酒时，要记得“倒茶要浅，倒酒要满”，这是表示对客人的尊重，也是显示主人的热情。

（本文选自百度百科词条“中式餐桌礼仪”，有改动）

Tips on Chinese Table Manners

1. **Seating**

The seating generally takes the left side as a symbol of honor and respect. Chinese banquet often uses a round table with the main seat facing the door. The closer to the main seat, the higher the status. For the same distance to the main seat, the left side is honored over the right side.

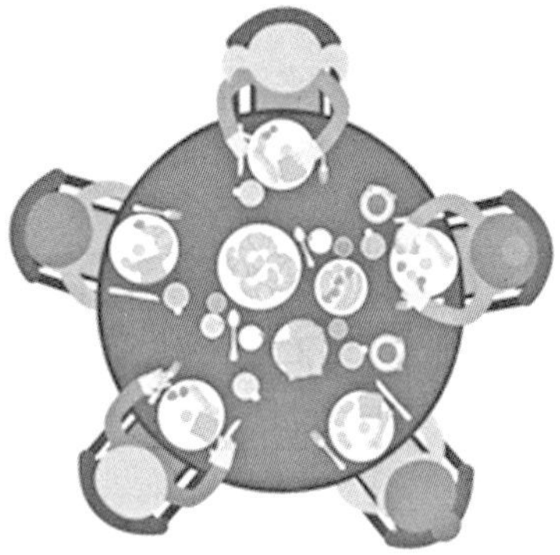

2. **Serving**

A Chinese meal usually starts with cold food (cold dishes, side dishes, etc.), then stir-fry, followed by the main course, and finally dim sum and soup. Now under the influence of Western food, desserts and fruits are often added at the end of the meal.

3. **Eating**

First invite the guests or elders to eat. Keep your voice down when eating and drinking soup so as not to disturb other people at the table. Some people like to make chewing noises when eating, which is very impolite. Pick only what's in front of you. It's rude to pick through the whole dish.

4. **Pouring tea and wine**

Chinese people love drinking tea, so tea usually is part of a Chinese banquet. When you pour tea and wine for others, remember to "fill the teacup partly and the wine cup full", which shows respect to the guests and displays the host's hospitality.

第六课

可以为您打扫房间吗

课前热身 Warming up

1. 你知道如何请酒店服务员打扫房间吗？

   Do you know how to ask a hotel attendant to clean a room?

2. 你们国家的酒店都提供哪些服务？

   What services are provided by hotels in your country?

课文 Text

李先生一家正准备出门，客房服务员正要来打扫房间。

Mr. Li and his family are about to go out, and the room attendant is coming to clean the room.

Lǐ Wěi
李 伟

中国商人

A business man from China

fúwùyuán
服务员

客房部服务员

a waitress of the

housekeeping department

Fúwùyuán: Nín hǎo, wǒ shì kèfáng fúwùyuán, kěyǐ wèi nín dǎsǎo fángjiān ma?
服务员：您 好，我 是 客房 服务员，可以 为 您 打扫 房间 吗？

Lǐ Wěi: Xūyào duō cháng shíjiān ne?
李 伟：需要 多 长 时间 呢？

Fúwùyuán: Bàn ge xiǎoshí zuǒyòu jiù kěyǐ le。
服务员：半 个 小时 左右 就 可以 了。

Lǐ Wěi: Nǐ néng bu néng xiàwǔ zài lái ne? Wǒmen xiànzài yào chūmén le。
李 伟：你 能 不 能 下午 再 来 呢？我们 现在 要 出门 了。

Fúwùyuán: Hǎo de。 Rúguǒ nín xiàwǔ xūyào dǎsǎo fángjiān, qǐng yòng
服务员：好的。如果您下午需要打扫房间，请用

fángjiān diànhuà bōdǎ yú kèfáng bù liánxì。
房间电话拨打“5”与客房部联系。

Zhù nín wán de kāixīn!
祝您玩得开心！

Lǐ Wěi: Hǎo de, xièxie。
李伟：好的，谢谢。

(Xiàwǔ lǐ xiānsheng hé jiārén huí dào jiǔdiàn hòu, gěi kèfáng bù dǎ le diànhuà。)
（下午李先生和家人回到酒店后，给客房部打了电话。）

Fúwùyuán: Nín hǎo, zhèlǐ shì kèfáng bù! Qǐngwèn yǒu shénme kěyǐ bāng nín?
服务员：您好，这里是客房部！请问有什么可以帮您？

Lǐ Wěi: Wǒ xiǎng qǐng nǐmen lái dǎsǎo yíxià fángjiān。
李伟：我想请你们来打扫一下房间。

Fúwùyuán: Hǎo de。Qǐng shāo děng, fúwùyuán mǎshàng guòqù。
服务员：好的。请稍等，服务员马上过去。

Lǐ Wěi: Xièxie!
李伟：谢谢！

(Shí fēn zhōng hòu, fúwùyuán qiāo mén。)
（十分钟后，服务员敲门。）

Fúwùyuán: Nín hǎo! Kèfáng fúwù。
服务员：您好！客房服务。

Lǐ tàitai: Nǐ hǎo, máfan nǐ le。
李太太：你好，麻烦你了。

Fúwùyuán：Nín tài kèqi le，zhè shì wǒ yīnggāi zuò de。
服务员：您 太 客气 了，这 是 我 应该 做 的。

Lǐ tàitai：Kěyǐ xiān dǎsǎo yùshì ma？
李 太太：可以 先 打扫 浴室 吗？

Fúwùyuán：Hǎo de。Zhèxiē máojīn hái yào yòng ma？
服务员：好 的。这些 毛巾 还 要 用 吗？

Lǐ tàitai：Huàn le ba。
李 太太：换 了 吧。

Fúwùyuán：Hǎo de。Xūyào xiànzài gěi nín xī chén ma？
服务员：好 的。…… 需要 现在 给 您 吸 尘 吗？

Lǐ Wěi：Xià cì ba。Xiànzài xī chén tài chǎo le。
李 伟：下 次 吧。现在 吸 尘 太 吵 了。

Fúwùyuán：Hǎo de。Xūyào bāng nín zhěnglǐ chuángpù ma？
服务员：好 的。需要 帮 您 整理 床铺 吗？

Lǐ Wěi：Qǐng huàn yíxià chuángdān hé zhěntào。
李 伟：请 换 一下 床单 和 枕套。

Fúwùyuán：Hǎo de。Qǐngwèn hái yǒu shénme xūyào ma？
服务员：好 的。请问 还 有 什么 需要 吗？

Lǐ tàitai：Yùshì de chuīfēngjī bú tài hǎo yòng，kěyǐ huàn yí gè xīn de ma？
李 太太：浴室 的 吹风机 不 太 好 用，可以 换 一 个 新 的 吗？

Fúwùyuán：Kěyǐ de，wǒ děng huìr gěi nín sòng lái。
服务员：可以 的，我 等 会儿 给 您 送 来。

Lǐ tàitai：Xièxie。
李 太太：谢谢。

Fúwùyuán：Bú kèqi。
服务员：不 客气。

生词 New words

1	打扫	dǎsǎo	动	to clean
2	时间	shíjiān	名	time
3	出门	chūmén	动	to go out
4	拨打	bōdǎ	动	to dail
5	麻烦	máfan	动	bother
6	应该	yīnggāi	动	should
7	浴室	yùshì	名	bathroom
8	毛巾	máojīn	名	towel
9	换	huàn	动	to change
10	吸尘	xī chén		to vacuum
11	吵	chǎo	形	noisy
12	床铺	chuángpù	名	bed
13	床单	chuángdān	名	bed sheets
14	枕套	zhěntào	名	pillowcase
15	吹风机	chuīfēngjī	名	hair dryer
16	新	xīn	形	new

语言点　Language points

1. "……就可以了"

just...

Dǎsǎo fángjiān xūyào duō cháng shíjiān?
(1) A：打扫 房间 需要 多 长 时间？

fēn zhōng jiù kěyǐ le。
B：30 分 钟 就 可以 了。

Cóng jiǔdiàn dào dìtiě zhàn yào duō jiǔ?
(2) A：从 酒店 到 地铁 站 要 多久？

Zǒulù fēn zhōng jiù kěyǐ le。
B：走路 10 分 钟 就 可以 了。

2. "如果……"

If...

Rúguǒ nín xūyào jìcún xíngli, kěyǐ dào jiǔdiàn qiántái zhǎo fúwùyuán。
(1) 如果 您 需要 寄存 行李，可以 到 酒店 前台 找 服务员。

Rúguǒ nín yào yòng xiànjīn zhīfù, zhǐ néng yòng měiyuán。
(2) 如果 您 要 用 现金 支付，只 能 用 美元。

Rúguǒ bùxiǎng xià lóu chī wǎncān, kěyǐ qǐng cāntīng sòng cān。
(3) 如果 不想 下 楼 吃 晚餐，可以 请 餐厅 送 餐。

3. “我可以……吗？”

May I…

Wǒ kěyǐ dǎsǎo yíxià yùshì ma?
(1) 我 可以 打扫 一下 浴室 吗？

Wǒ kěyǐ xiànzài xī chén ma?
(2) 我 可以 现在 吸 尘 吗？

Wǒ kěyǐ huàn yí gè xīn de ma?
(3) 我 可以 换 一 个 新 的 吗？

练习 Exercises

1. 看图片说词。

Speak out the words according to the pictures.

(1) ________________

(2) ________________

（3）________

（4）________

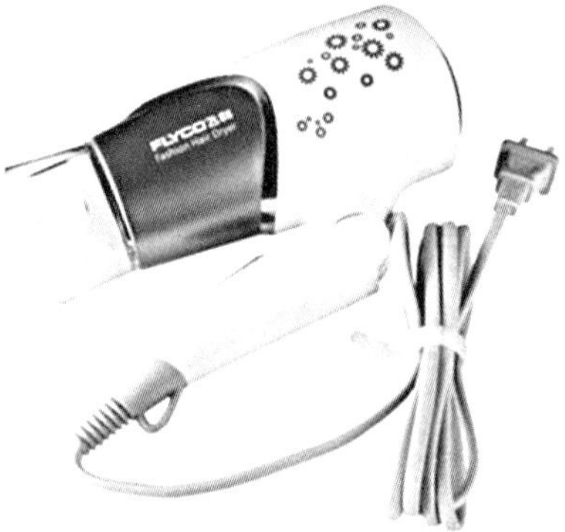

（5）________

（6）________

2. 短语连线，并完成句子。

Match the words and complete the sentences.

打扫	入住	换	拨打	吸	整理
毛巾	尘	床铺	愉快	房间	电话

xūyào xiànzài gěi nín ma?
(1) 需要 现在 给 您 ________ 吗?

Nǐ hǎo, kěyǐ qǐng fúwùyuán lái ma? Wǒ de fángjiān
(2) 你 好,可以 请 服务员 来 ________ 吗? 我 的 房间

yǒudiǎnr luàn。
有点儿 乱。(in a mess)

Lǐ xiānsheng, zhè shì nín de fángkǎ, zhù nín
(3) 李 先生, 这 是 您 的 房卡, 祝 您 ________。

Wǒmen jiǔdiàn de yùshì měi tiān dōu huì
(4) 我们 酒店 的 浴室 每 天 都 会 ________。

Rúguǒ xiǎng zài fángjiān yòngcān, kěyǐ dào cānyǐn
(5) 如果 想 在 房间 用餐, 可以 ________ 到 餐饮

bù, ràng tāmen gěi nín sòng cān。
部, 让 他们 给 您 送 餐。

Rúguǒ nín bù xūyào qǐng gàosu kèfáng fúwùyuán。
(6) 如果 您 不 需要 ________, 请 告诉 客房 服务员。

3. 根据要求,完成对话。

Complete the conversations.

Nǐ hǎo, kèfáng fúwù,
(1) A: 你 好, 客房 服务, ________?

Hǎo de, qǐng jìn。Dǎsǎo fángjiān xūyào duō cháng shíjiān ne?
B: 好 的, 请 进。打扫 房间 需要 多 长 时间 呢?

A: ________。

Hǎo de, nà wǒmen děng nǐ dǎsǎo wán zài chūmén ba。
B: 好 的,那 我们 等 你 打扫 完 再 出门 吧。

Wèi, qiántái, wǒ shì fáng de, wǒ fángjiān li de chuīfēngjī bú
(2) A: 喂, 前台, 我 是 1001 房 的, 我 房间 里 的 吹风机 不

tài hǎo yòng, kěyǐ huàn yí gè ma?
太好用，可以换一个吗？

Hǎo de,
B：好的，＿＿＿＿＿＿＿＿＿＿＿＿＿＿＿＿＿。

Hái yǒu, kěyǐ qǐng rén lái dǎsǎo yíxià fángjiān ma?
A：还有，可以请人来打扫一下房间吗？

Hǎo de。Rúguǒ nín xūyào kèfáng dǎsǎo, kěyǐ
B：好的。如果您需要客房打扫，可以＿＿＿＿＿＿＿＿＿＿。

4. 情景练习。

Practice speaking.

你是客房部的服务员，你进入房间打扫时，客人回来了，想请你尽快完成打扫，他们想休息。你应该怎么说呢？

You are an attendant of the housekeeping department. When you enter the room for cleaning, the guests come back. They ask you to finish the cleaning as soon as possible, because they want to have a rest. What should you say?

小知识 Notes

客房清扫注意事项

（1）整理房间时，要将房门打开。

（2）客人衣服不能移动，必要时轻拿轻放。

（3）客人退房后，如发现现金和首饰应做好记录并及时告知上级。

（4）不随意触摸客人的照相机、电脑、手机和钱包等物品。

（5）清扫时，将客人的文件、杂志、书报等稍加整理，不能翻看。

（6）除放在垃圾桶里的东西外，其他东西不能自行丢掉。

（7）化妆品可以稍加整理，但不要移动位置。

（8）损坏客人物品，应赔礼道歉，如需赔偿，应由客房部出面进行协商。

（9）离开房间时，应打开房内照明灯。

（本文选自百度文库：《客房清扫应注意哪些问题》，有改动）

Housekeeping Notes

(1) Leave the door open when tidying up the room.

(2) Do not move the guest's clothes. Handle it carefully if necessary.

(3) If cash and jewelry are found after the guests check out, make records

and inform the superiors in time.

(4) Do not touch guests' cameras, computers, mobile phones, wallets and other items at will.

(5) The guests' documents, magazines, books and newspapers shall be slightly sorted out and shall not be read.

(6) Don't throw away anything except the things in the trash can.

(7) The cosmetics can be slightly tidied up, but shall not be moved.

(8) In case of damage to the guest's things, an apology shall be made. If compensation is needed, the Housekeeping Department shall negotiate.

(9) Turn on the lights in the room when leaving the room.

第七课

您有衣服要送洗吗

课前热身 Warming up

1. 你知道如何填写洗衣单吗？

   Do you know how to fill out a laundry form?

2. 你知道"快洗"和"隔日取"的区别吗？

   Do you know the difference between "quick wash" and "pick up every other day"?

课文 Text

李先生有几件衣服想要送洗，他拨打客服电话，请客房服务员提供衣服送洗服务。

Some clothes of Mr. Li need to be washed. He calls customer service and asks the room attendant to provide laundry service.

Lǐ Wěi
李 伟

中国商人

A business man from China

fúwùyuán
服务员

客房部服务员

a waitress of the

housekeeping department

Fúwùyuán：Nín hǎo！Zhèlǐ shì kèfáng bù。
服务员：您 好！这里 是 客房 部。

Lǐ Wěi：Wǒ yǒu jǐ jiàn yīfu yào xǐ，nǐmen yǒu yīfu sòng xǐ fúwù ma？
李 伟：我 有 几 件 衣服 要 洗，你们 有 衣服 送 洗 服务 吗？

Fúwùyuán：Xiānsheng，wǒmen tígōng yīfu sòng xǐ de。
服务员：先生，我们 提供 衣服 送 洗 的。

Xūyào xiànzài dào nín de fángjiān qù ná yīfu ma？
需要 现在 到 您 的 房间 去 拿 衣服 吗？

Lǐ Wěi：xiànzài jiù lái ba。
李 伟：现在 就 来 吧。

(Shí fēn zhōng hòu, kèfáng fúwùyuán lái dào Lǐ xiānsheng de fángjiān。)
(十 分 钟 后，客房 服务员 来 到 李 先生 的 房间。)

Fúwùyuán: Nín hǎo! Nín xūyào yīfu sòng xǐ ma?
服务员：您 好！您 需要 衣服 送 洗 吗？

Lǐ Wěi: Shì de, qǐng jìn!
李 伟：是 的，请 进！

Fúwùyuán: Nín néng tián yíxià xǐ yī dān ma?
服务员：您 能 填 一下 洗 衣 单 吗？

Xǐ yī dān zài chōuti lǐ。
洗 衣 单 在 抽屉 里。

Lǐ Wěi: Hǎo de。 Duìle, zhè liǎng jiàn chènyī kěyǐ bāng wǒ yùn yíxià ma?
李 伟：好 的。……对了，这 两 件 衬衣 可以 帮 我 熨 一下 吗？

Fúwùyuán: Dāngrán kěyǐ, nín kěyǐ zài xǐ yī dān shàng xiě yíxià nǎ jiàn yīfu xūyào yùn。
服务员：当然 可以，您 可以 在 洗 衣 单 上 写 一下 哪 件 衣服 需要 熨。

Lǐ Wěi: Hǎo de。
李 伟：好 的。

(Fúwùyuán rènzhēn jiǎnchá kèrén de yīfu hé xǐ yī dān。)
(服务员 认真 检查 客人 的 衣服 和 洗 衣 单。)

Fúwùyuán: Nín yígòng sòng xǐ sān jiàn yīfu, liǎng jiàn chènyī, yì tiáo kùzi。
服务员：您 一共 送 洗 三 件 衣服，两 件 衬衣，一 条 裤子。

Lǐ Wěi: Shénme shíhou néng sòng huílái ne?
李 伟：什么 时候 能 送 回来 呢？

Fúwùyuán: Wǒmen yǒu gérì qǔ hé kuài xǐ, nín xūyào nǎ zhǒng?
服务员：我们 有 隔日 取 和 快 洗，您 需要 哪 种？

Lǐ　Wěi：Jiàgé bù yíyàng ma?
李　伟：价格 不 一样 吗?

Fúwùyuán：Shìde，gérì qǔ，měi jiàn yīfu　měiyuán。kuài xǐ de huà，měi
服务员：是的，隔日 取，每 件 衣服 10 美元。快 洗 的 话，每

jiàn yīfu　měiyuán，zhǐyào　gè xiǎoshí jiù néng xǐ hǎo。
件 衣服 15 美元，只要 3 个 小时 就 能 洗 好。

Lǐ　Wěi：Rúguǒ gérì qǔ，míngtiān jǐ diǎn sòng huílái ne？
李　伟：如果 隔日 取，明天 几 点 送 回来 呢?

Fúwùyuán：Shàngwǔ　diǎn zhīqián。
服务员：上午 8 点 之前。

Lǐ　Wěi：Nà jiù gérì qǔ ba。
李　伟：那 就 隔日 取 吧。

Fúwùyuán：Hǎo de。
服务员：好 的。

生词　New words

1	衣服	yīfu	名	clothes
2	洗	xǐ	动	to wash，to clean
3	件	jiàn	量	piece
4	服务	fúwù	动	service
5	提供	tígōng	动	to offer，to provide
6	洗衣单	xǐ yī dān		laundry list

7	抽屉	chōuti	名	drawer
8	衬衣	chènyī	名	shirt
9	熨	yùn	动	to iron
10	当然	dāngrán	形	of course, sure
11	认真	rènzhēn	形	carefully
12	检查	jiǎnchá	动	to check
13	裤子	kùzi	名	trousers
14	快洗	kuài xǐ		quick wash
15	隔日	gérì	动	next day
16	取	qǔ	动	to get, to pick up
17	价格	jiàgé	名	price
18	每	měi	代	every
19	只要	zhǐyào	连	as long as
20	之前	zhīqián	名	before

语言点　Language points

1. “……的话，……就……”
if…, then…

Kuài xǐ de huà, gè xiǎoshí jiù hǎo le。
(1) 快 洗 的 话，3 个 小时 就 好 了。

Gérì qǔ de huà, míngtiān shàngwǔ diǎn zhīqián jiù sòng huí。
(2) 隔日 取 的 话， 明天 上午 8 点 之前 就 送 回。

Méiyǒu yùdìng de huà, nín jiù bù néng bànlǐ rùzhù。
(3) 没有 预订 的 话，您 就 不 能 办理 入住。

2. “只要……就……”
as long as…

Zhǐyào dǎ diànhuà dào kèfáng bù, fúwùyuán jiù lái wèi nín dǎsǎo fángjiān。
(1) 只要 打 电话 到 客房 部，服务员 就 来 为 您 打扫 房间。

Zhǐyào shì jiǔdiàn de kèrén, jiù kěyǐ miǎnfèi chī zǎocān。
(2) 只要 是 酒店 的 客人，就 可以 免费 吃 早餐。

3. “……吗”

语气词，用在句末，表示疑问。

Modal particle “吗” is used at the end of a sentence to form a question.

Wǒ kěyǐ yòng xiànjīn zhīfù ma?
(1) 我 可以 用 现金 支付 吗？

Qǐngwèn, diǎn zhīqián wǒ kěyǐ tuì fáng ma?
(2) 请问，10 点 之前 我 可以 退 房 吗？

练习 Exercises

1. 看图片说词。

Speak out the words according to the pictures.

 (1) ________	 (2) ________

 (3) ________	 (4) ________
 (5) ________	 (6) ________

2. 短语连线，并完成句子。

Match the words and complete the sentences.

送洗	填	熨	隔日	一条	确认
价格	裤子	服务	洗衣单	衣服	取

Nín yígòng sòng xǐ sān jiàn yīfu, liǎngjiàn chènyī,
(1) 您 一共 送 洗 三 件 衣服，两件 衬衣，________________________。

jiùshì dì èr tiān zài bǎ yīfu sòng huílái。
(2) ____________________就是 第 二 天 再 把 衣服 送 回来。

Sòng xǐ yīfu shí, qǐng xiān
(3) 送 洗 衣服 时，请 先____________________。

Nǐhǎo! qǐngwèn nǐmen yǒu yīfu ma?
(4) 你好！ 请问 你们 有 衣服____________________吗？

Rúguǒ kèrén xūyào, kèrén kěyǐ zìjǐ
(5) 如果 客人 需要，客人 可以 自己____________________。

Sòng xǐ yīfu de shíhou, qǐng hé shùliàng。
(6) 送 洗 衣服 的 时候，请____________________和 数量。

3. 根据要求，完成对话。

Complete the conversations.

Nǐhǎo, kèfáng fúwù,
(1) A：你好，客房 服务，____________________？

Shì de, wǒ yǒu yīfu yào xǐ。
B：是 的，我 有 衣服 要 洗。

A：______________________________？

Xǐ yī dān zài nǎlǐ?
B：洗 衣 单 在 哪里？

A：______________________________。

Yīfu xǐ hǎo hòu shénme shíhou sòng huílái ne?
(2) A：衣服 洗 好 后 什么 时候 送 回来 呢？

nín yào nǎ yì zhǒng ne?
B：____________________，您 要 哪 一 种 呢？

Kuài xǐ duōshao qián?
A：快 洗 多 少　钱？

dànshì zhǐyào　xiǎoshí jiù hǎole。
B：____________，但是　只要 3　小时　就 好了。

Nà jiù yào kuài xǐ ba。
A：那 就 要　快　洗 吧。

4. 情景练习。

Practice speaking.

你是客房部的服务员，你进入房间打扫时，客人把一袋衣服交给你，请你送洗，并要求明天送回来。你应该怎么跟他说？

You are a room attendant. When you enter the room to clean, the guest gives you a bag of clothes for laundry service and requests the clothes be sent back tomorrow. What should you tell him?

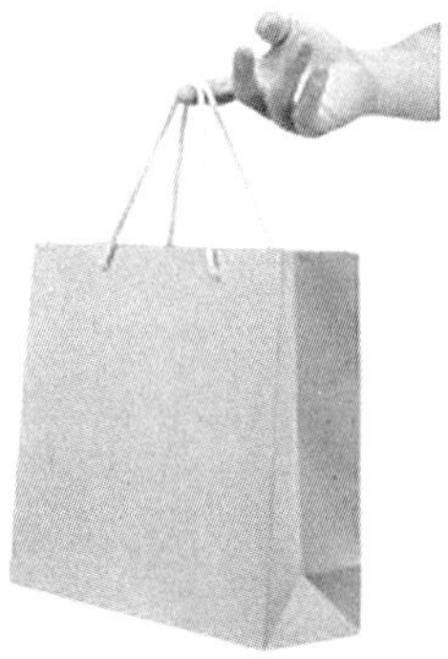

小知识 Notes

酒店服务

酒店接待服务，包括停车、行李运送、翻译、外币兑换、贵重物品存放、各种会议接待等。

酒店客房服务，包括客房出租、客房保险柜、冷热水供应、电视网络、客房酒水服务、洗衣熨烫服务以及叫醒服务等。

酒店餐饮服务，主要提供中餐、西餐、风味餐、自助餐、宴会、酒会、咖啡厅、酒吧以及客房送餐等。

酒店娱乐服务，主要提供保龄球、网球、游泳、健身、美容、美发、按摩、牌类、棋类、电子游戏等。

酒店商场服务，主要是向客人提供食品、纪念品、图书、文化用品以及服装等。

酒店其他服务，包括旅游汽车出租、幼儿托管、宠物托管等。

（本文选自百度环球网校：《酒店服务有哪些》，有改动）

Hotel Services

Hotel reception services include parking, luggage delivery, translation services, foreign currency exchange services, valuables storage services, various conference reception services, etc.

Hotel housekeeping services include room rental, in-room safe supply, hot and cold water supply, television and internet supply, beverages service, laundry and ironing service and wake-up call service.

Hotel catering services mainly provide Chinese food, Western food, special flavour food, buffets, banquets, cocktail parties, cafes, bars and room delivery services.

Hotel entertainment services mainly provide bowling, tennis, swimming, fitness, beauty, hairdressing, massage, cards, chess and video games.

Hotel shopping mall services mainly provide guests with food, souvenirs, books, cultural goods and clothing.

Other services of the hotel include tourist car rental, child care, pet care, etc.

第八课

麻烦您登记一下房号和姓名

课前热身 Warming up

1. 你们国家的酒店有“康体中心”吗？

   Do hotels in your country have fitness centers?

2. 你知道“康体中心”都有哪些服务吗？

   Do you know what services are available at the fitness center?

课文 Text

李先生想到酒店的健身房锻炼锻炼，他来到酒店康体中心进行咨询。

Mr. Li wants to work out at the hotel gym, so he goes to the hotel fitness center for a consultation.

Lǐ Wěi
李 伟

中国商人

A business man from China

fúwùyuán
服务员

康体中心服务员

a waitress of the hotel fitness center

Fúwùyuán：Zǎoshang hǎo，huānyíng guānglín kāng tǐ zhōngxīn!
服务员：早上 好，欢迎 光临 康 体 中心！

Lǐ Wěi：Zǎoshang hǎo，wǒ tīngshuō zhèlǐ yǒu kāng tǐ zhōngxīn，jiù guòlái kàn kan。
李 伟：早上 好，我 听说 这里 有 康 体 中心，就 过来 看 看。

Fúwùyuán：Hǎo de。Wǒmen jiǔdiàn de kāng tǐ zhōngxīn yǒu jiànshēnfáng hé yóuyǒngchí，hái yǒu sāngná hé ànmó fúwù，nín dōu kěyǐ tǐyàn
服务员：好 的。我们 酒店 的 康 体 中心 有 健身房 和 游泳池，还 有 桑拿 和 按摩 服务，您 都 可以 体验

yíxià。
一下。

Lǐ Wěi：Wǒ xiǎng duànliàn duànliàn，xiān pǎo pǎobù。
李 伟：我 想 锻炼 锻炼，先 跑 跑步。

Fúwùyuán：Hǎo de。Máfan nín xiān dēngjì yíxià fáng hào hé xìngmíng。
服务员：好 的。麻烦 您 先 登记 一下 房 号 和 姓名。

Lǐ Wěi：Hǎo de。Zài zhèlǐ yùndòng xūyào fù qián ma？
李 伟：好 的。在 这里 运动 需要 付 钱 吗？

Fúwùyuán：Jiànshēnfáng duì jiǔdiàn kèrén shì miǎnfèi de。
服务员：健身房 对 酒店 客人 是 免费 的。

Lǐ Wěi：Yǒu shíjiān xiànzhì ma？
李 伟：有 时间 限制 吗？

Fúwùyuán：Cóng zǎoshang diǎn dào wǎnshang diǎn。
服务员：从 早上 9 点 到 晚上 9 点。

Lǐ Wěi：Yǒu nǎxiē jiànshēn qìcái？
李 伟：有 哪些 健身 器材？

Fúwùyuán：Yǒu pǎobùjī、yùndòng dānchē、yǎlíng děng jiànshēn qìcái。
服务员：有 跑步机、运动 单车、哑铃 等 健身 器材。

Shǐyòng qián zuìhǎo xiān zuò shēnzhǎn yùndòng。
使用 前 最好 先 做 伸展 运动。

Lǐ Wěi：Hǎo de。Wǒ xiān yòng yíxià pǎobùjī ba。
李 伟：好 的。我 先 用 一下 跑步机 吧。

Fúwùyuán：Rúguǒ nín yǒu shénme wèntí，kěyǐ suíshí jiào wǒ。Wǒ hěn lèyì
服务员：如果 您 有 什么 问题，可以 随时 叫 我。我 很 乐意

wèi nín fúwù。
为 您 服务。

Lǐ Wěi：Hǎo de，xièxie！
李 伟：好 的，谢谢！

生词　New words

1	健身房	jiànshēnfáng	名	gym
2	锻炼	duànliàn	动	to exercise
3	康体中心	kāng tǐ zhōngxīn		fitness center
4	听说	tīngshuō	动	hear of
5	游泳池	yóuyǒngchí	名	swimming pool
6	桑拿	sāngná	名	sauna
7	按摩	ànmó	动	massage
8	体验	tǐyàn	动	experience, try
9	跑步	pǎobù	动	to run
10	登记	dēngjì	动	to register
11	免费	miǎnfèi	形	free
12	限制	xiànzhì	名	limitation
13	器材	qìcái	名	equipment
14	跑步机	pǎobùjī	名	treadmill

15	运动单车	yùndòng dānchē		spinning
16	哑铃	yǎlíng	名	dumbbell
17	最	zuì	副	most
18	伸展	shēnzhǎn	动	to stretch
19	随时	suíshí	副	at any time
20	乐意	lèyì	形	willing

语言点 Language points

1. “有……，还有……”

have...and...

Jiǔdiàn zǎocān yǒu sānmíngzhì hé shālā, hái yǒu gè zhǒng miànbāo。
(1) 酒店早餐有三明治和沙拉，还有各种面包。

Wǒmen jiǔdiàn yǒu dān rén fáng, háiyǒu shuāng rén jiān。
(2) 我们酒店有单人间，还有双人间。

2. "……最好……"

You'd better do sth.

Shǐyòng pǎobùjī qián zuìhǎo xiān zuò shēnzhǎn yùndòng。
(1) 使用 跑步机 前 最好 先 做 伸展 运动。

Chūxíng qián zuìhǎo xiān yùdìng jiǔdiàn。
(2) 出行 前 最好 先 预订 酒店。

Tuì fáng qián zuìhǎo xiān jiǎnchá yíxià fángjiān。
(3) 退 房 前 最好 先 检查 一下 房间。

3. "动词重叠"

Verb reduplication

"看看"表示时间短，单音节动词重叠 AA 式。

The reduplication form of monosyllabic verbs is AA, which indicates short duration.

"锻炼锻炼"表示时间短，双音节动词重叠 ABAB 式。

The reduplication form of disyllabic verbs is ABAB, which indicates short duration.

Nín kàn kan hái xūyào qítā fúwù ma?
(1) 您 看 看 还 需要 其他 服务 吗?

Nín kěyǐ kàn kan shū、tīng ting yīnyuè。
(2) 您 可以 看 看 书、听 听 音乐。

Nín kěyǐ qù jiànshēnfáng duànliàn duànliàn shēntǐ, ránhòu zài huí kèfáng xiūxi。
(3) 您 可以 去 健身房 锻炼 锻炼 身体，然后 再 回 客房 休息。

4. “从……到……”

From...to...

Cóng diǎn dào diǎn shì jiǔdiàn de zǎocān shíjiān。
(1) 从 6 点 到 10 点 是 酒店 的 早餐 时间。

Cóng kèfáng dào xǐshǒujiān dōu hěn gānjìng。
(2) 从 客房 到 洗手间 都 很 干净。(clean)

练习　Exercises

1. 看图片说词。

Speak out the words according to the pictures.

(1) ________________

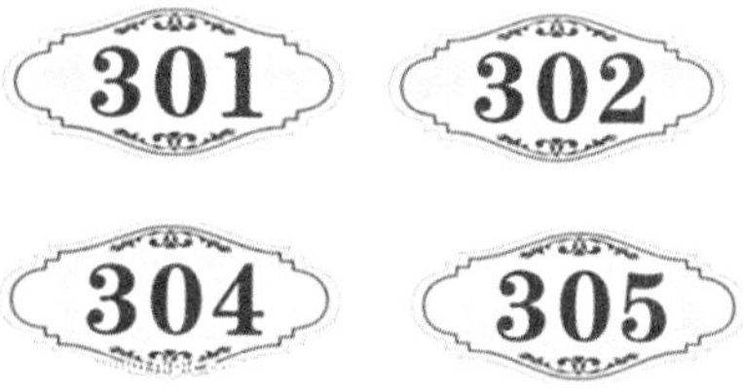

(2) ________________

(3) ________________

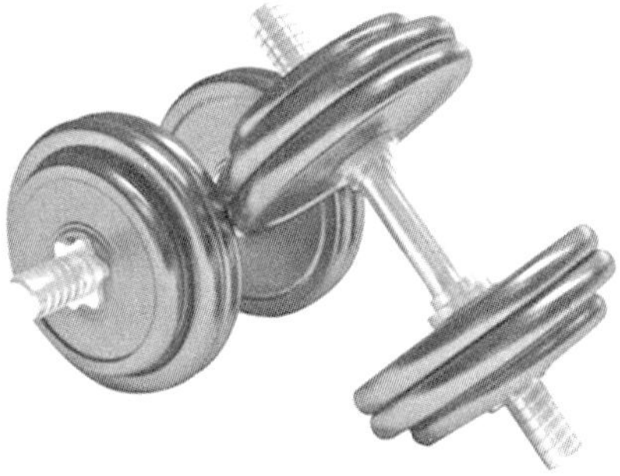

(4) ________________

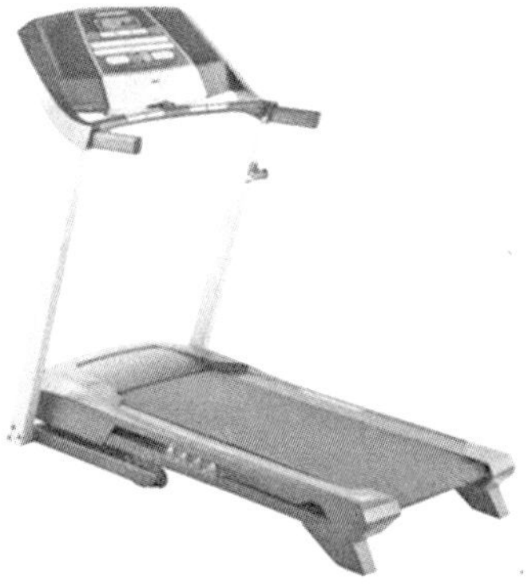	
(5) ______	(6) ______

2. 短语连线，并完成句子。

Match the words and complete the sentences.

锻炼	登记	按摩	免费	健身	伸展
器材	身体	房号	服务	运动	开放

(Example: 锻炼 — 身体)

Qù cāntīng chī zìzhùcān de shíhou, qǐng xiān
(1) 去 餐厅 吃 自助餐 的 时候，请 先 ______。

Wǒmen de jiànshēn zhōngxīn duì jiǔdiàn kèrén
(2) 我们 的 健身 中心 对 酒店 客人 ______。

Rúguǒ nín shì dì-yī cì lái, shǐyòng ______ de shíhou yào zhùyì ānquán。
(3) 如果 您 是 第一次 来，使用 ______ 的 时候 要 注意 安全。

Qǐngwèn jiǔdiàn yǒu jiànshēnfáng ma? Wǒ xiǎng
(4) 请问 酒店 有 健身房 吗? 我 想 ______________。

Wǒmen jiǔdiàn de hěn búcuò, nín yùndòng hòu kěyǐ
(5) 我们 酒店 的 ______________ 很 不错，您 运动 后 可以

lái fàngsōng yíxià。
来 放松 一下。

Pǎobù qián zuìhǎo xiān zuò
(6) 跑步 前 最好 先 做 ______________。

3. 根据要求，完成对话。

Complete the conversations.

Nǐ hǎo, huānyíng guānglín kāng tǐ zhōngxīn,
(1) A：你 好， 欢迎 光临 康 体 中心， ______________？

Wǒ xiǎng pǎo pǎobù。
B：我 想 跑 跑步。

Hǎo de, fáng hào hé xìngmíng。
A：好 的， ______________________ 房 号 和 姓名。

Zài zhèlǐ yùndòng yào fù qián ma?
(2) A：在 这里 运动 要 付 钱 吗？

Búyòng fù qián, zhǐyào shì
B：不用 付 钱， __________________________， 只要 是

kèrén jiù kěyǐ lái yùndòng。
客人 就 可以 来 运动。

4. 情景练习。

Practice speaking.

你是康体中心的服务员，每天都有不同的客人来运动，请你设计一段

话，向他们介绍康体中心的服务项目。

You are the attendant of the fitness center. Every day, different guests come here to do exercises. Please design a guide to introduce the services of the center to them.

小知识 Notes

按摩知多少

按摩是中国最古老的医疗方法之一，又称推拿。按摩对身体有很多益处，它可以放松肌肉、减轻压力、缓解疲劳等。

按摩有保健类按摩和治疗类按摩。保健类按摩有美容按摩、减肥按摩、足部按摩等；治疗性按摩主要有火罐、刮痧、艾灸等。“火罐”又称“拔火罐”，根据患者病情而定，一般为 10 ~ 15 分钟。刮痧根据部位不同和刮痧面积，价格也从几十元到几百元不等。艾灸的治疗范围很广，对于肩周炎、颈椎病、胃痛等常见疾病都有很好的治疗效果。

除了中式按摩外，泰式按摩、日式指压按摩等也是有名的按摩方式。

（本文选自百度百科词条“按摩”，有改动）

How Much do You Know about Massage

Massage is the oldest medical treatment in China, also known as Tui Na（推拿）. Massage has many benefits for the body. It can relax muscles, reduce stress and relieve fatigue.

Massage includes health care massage and therapeutic massage. Health – care massage includes beauty massage, weight – loss massage, foot massage, etc. Therapeutic massage mainly includes cupping, scraping, moxibustion, etc. “Cupping”, also known as “fire cupping”, usually lasts for 10 – 15 minutes depending on the patient's condition. The price of scraping varies from dozens to hundreds of yuan according to the different parts and areas of scraping. Moxibustion can treat a wide range of health conditions, and has a good therapeutic effect on scapulohumeral periarthritis, cervical spondylosis, stomachache and other common diseases.

Besides Chinese massage, Thai massage and Japanese shiatsu massage are also very famous massage styles.

第九课

我们酒店有天际泳池

课前热身 Warming up

1. 你知道什么是“室外天际泳池”吗?

   Do you know what an outdoor skyline swimming pool is?

2. 在室内游泳需要注意什么?

   What do you need to pay attention to when swimming indoors?

课文 Text

今天天气比较热，李先生想去游泳池游泳，他来到康体中心询问。

It is hot today. Mr. Li wants to swim in the swimming pool. He goes to the health center to ask for more information.

Lǐ Wěi
李 伟
中国商人
A business man from China

fúwùyuán
服务员
康体中心服务员
a waitress of the hotel fitness center

Fúwùyuán: Xiàwǔ hǎo, huānyíng guānglín kāng tǐ zhōngxīn!
服务员：下午 好，欢迎 光临 康 体 中心！

Lǐ Wěi: Xiàwǔ hǎo, tīngshuō nǐmen jiǔdiàn de yóuyǒngchí búcuò, wǒ xiǎng lái shì shi。
李 伟：下午 好，听说 你们 酒店 的 游泳池 不错，我 想 来 试 试。

Fúwùyuán: Hǎo de, wǒmen jiǔdiàn yǒu yí gè shì nèi héngwēn yǒngchí hé yí gè shì wài tiānjì yǒngchí, qǐngwèn nín xiǎng qù nǎ yí gè?
服务员：好 的，我们 酒店 有 一 个 室 内 恒温 泳池 和 一 个 室 外 天际 泳池，请问 您 想 去 哪 一 个？

Lǐ Wěi：Tiānjì yǒngchí? Jiùshì nàge wǎng hóng yóuyǒngchí ma？
李　伟：天际 泳池？ 就是 那个 网 红 游泳池 吗？

Fúwùyuán：Shì de，wǒmen de tiānjì yǒngchí fēicháng yǒumíng，jīngcháng yǒu
服务员：是 的，我们 的 天际 泳池 非常 有名， 经常 有
yóukè lái pāizhào。
游客 来 拍照。

Lǐ Wěi：Nà jiù yào shì shi le。Búguò wǒ bú tài huì yóuyǒng。Shuǐ shēn yǒu
李　伟：那 就 要 试 试 了。不过 我 不 太 会 游泳。 水 深 有
duōshao mǐ ne?
多少 米 呢？

Fúwùyuán：Zuì shēn de dìfang yǒu liǎng mǐ，nín kěyǐ zài qiǎn shuǐ qū，nàlǐ
服务员：最 深 的 地方 有 两 米，您 可以 在 浅 水 区，那里
zhǐyǒu mǐ。
只有 1.5 米。

Lǐ Wěi：Hǎo de。Duìle，nǐmen zhèlǐ jǐ diǎn guānmén?
李　伟：好 的。对了，你们 这里 几 点 关门？

Fúwùyuán：Shì wài yǒngchí cóng zǎoshang diǎn dào xiàwǔ diǎn，shì nèi
服务员：室 外 泳池 从 早上 6 点 到 下午 6 点， 室 内
yǒngchí cóng zǎoshang diǎn dào wǎnshang diǎn。
泳池 从 早上 6 点 到 晚上 9 点。

Lǐ Wěi：Tài hǎole，nà wǒ qù tiānjì yǒngchí kàn kan fēngjǐng，ránhòu zài dào
李　伟：太 好了，那 我 去 天际 泳池 看 看 风景， 然后 再 到
shì nèi yǒngchí yóuyǒng。
室 内 泳池 游泳。

Fúwùyuán：Hǎo de。Zài shì nèi yǒngchí yóuyǒng de huà yào dài yǒng mào。
服务员：好 的。在 室 内 泳池 游泳 的 话 要 戴 泳 帽。

Lǐ Wěi：Āiya，wǒ méiyǒu yǒng mào，zěnme bàn?
李　伟：哎呀，我 没有 泳 帽， 怎么 办？

Fúwùyuán：Nín kěyǐ zài zhèlǐ mǎi yì dǐng， kuài qián yì dǐng。
服务员：您 可以 在 这里 买 一 顶，30 块 钱 一 顶。

Lǐ Wěi：Hǎo ba，nà gěi wǒ yì dǐng ba。
李　伟：好 吧，那 给 我 一 顶 吧。

Fúwùyuán: Hǎo de, zhè shì nín de yǒng mào。 Wǎng qián zǒu jiùshì gēngyīshì,
服务员：好的，这是您的泳帽。往前走就是更衣室，

zhè shì yàoshi。 Zhù nín wán de yúkuài!
这是钥匙。祝您玩得愉快！

生词 New words

1	天际	tiānjì	名	skyline
2	泳池	yǒngchí	名	swimming pool
3	试	shì	动	to try
4	室内	shì nèi		indoor
5	恒温	héngwēn	名	constant temperature
6	室外	shì wài		outdoor
7	网红	wǎng hóng		internet celebrity, influencer
8	有名	yǒumíng	形	famous
9	游客	yóukè	名	tourist
10	拍照	pāizhào	动	to take photo
11	水深	shuǐ shēn		water depth

12	浅水区	qiǎn shuǐ qū		shallow water area
13	关门	guānmén	动	to close the door
14	风景	fēngjǐng	名	scenery
15	戴	dài	动	to wear
16	泳帽	yǒng mào		swimming cap
17	顶	dǐng	量	top（a measure word）
18	往	wǎng	介	toward，to
19	钥匙	yàoshi	名	key

语言点 Language points

1. "……非常有名。"
…is very famous.

Wǒmen de tiānjì yǒngchí fēicháng yǒumíng。
(1) 我们 的 天际 泳池 非常 有名。

Wǒmen de niúnǎn miàn fēicháng yǒumíng。
(2) 我们 的 牛腩 面 非常 有名。

Wǒmen de jiǔdiàn fēicháng yǒumíng。
(3) 我们 的 酒店 非常 有名。

2. “往……走就是……”

go…and you will find…

Wǎng qián zǒu jiùshì gēngyīshì。
(1) 往 前 走 就是 更衣室。

Wǎng zuǒ zǒu jiùshì nín de fángjiān。
(2) 往 左 走 就是 您 的 房间。

Wǎng yòu zǒu jiùshì cāntīng。
(3) 往 右 走 就是 餐厅。

练习 Exercises

1. 看图片说词。

Speak out the words according to the pictures.

(1) ________________

(2) ________________

 (3) ________	 (4) ________
 (5) ________	 (6) ________

2. 短语连线，并完成句子。

Match the words and complete the sentences.

看	戴	室内	水深	拍	开放
泳池	照片	风景	泳帽	时间	两米

Nín de fángjiān zài gāocéng, zuì shìhé ________ le。
（1）您的房间在高层，最适合________了。

Wǒmen jiǔdiàn de ________ shì héngwēn de。
（2）我们酒店的________是恒温的。

Wǒmen de tiānjì yǒngchí fēicháng yǒumíng, jīngcháng yǒu yóukè lái ________。
（3）我们的天际泳池非常有名，经常有游客来________。

Zài shì nèi yǒngchí yóuyǒng de huà yào ________。
（4）在室内泳池游泳的话要________。

Jiǔdiàn de shì nèi yóuyǒngchí ________, rúguǒ nín bú tài huì yóuyǒng, kěyǐ dào qiǎn shuǐ qū。
（5）酒店的室内游泳池________，如果您不太会游泳，可以到浅水区。

Yóuyǒngchí de ________ shì cóng zǎoshang 6 diǎn dào xiàwǔ 6 diǎn。
（6）游泳池的________是从早上6点到下午6点。

3. 根据要求，完成对话。

Complete the conversations.

（1）A：Nǐ hǎo, huānyíng guānglín kāng tǐ zhōngxīn。
你好，欢迎光临康体中心。

B：Nǐ hǎo, nǐmen yǒu yóuyǒngchí ma?
你好，你们有游泳池吗？

A：Yǒu de, ________。
有的，________。

B：Yǒu duō shēn ne?
有多深呢？

A：________。

Jiǔdiàn de yóuyǒngchí jǐ diǎn guānmén?
（2）A：酒店 的 游泳池 几 点 关门？

B：______________________________________。

Xūyào dài yǒng mào ma?
A：需要 戴 泳 帽 吗？

Shì de, rúguǒ méiyǒu de huà,
B：是 的，______________________，如果 没有 的 话，

kuài qián yì dǐng。
______________________，30 块 钱 一 顶。

4. 情景练习。

Practice speaking.

你是酒店游泳池的管理员。今天酒店来了一个旅行团，一共 10 个大人 5 个小孩，他们想到游泳池游泳，请你向他们介绍进入泳池前的注意事项。

You are in charge of the hotel swimming pool. There is a group of 10 adults and 5 children coming to the hotel today. They want to swim in the swimming pool. Please introduce the precautions of the swimming pool to them.

小知识 Notes

休闲潜水

休闲潜水是指以水下观光和休闲娱乐为目的的潜水活动，分为浮潜和水肺潜水，很多海滨旅游景区都有潜水体验休闲项目。

在景区，一般是由教练带领游客下海体验潜水活动，深度通常不会超过 12 米。即使不会游泳，也可以享受潜水的乐趣。如果想自由潜水，必须要有潜水证。

三亚是中国非常有名的潜水胜地，拥有 19 家潜水俱乐部，26 个潜水点，每年有超过 100 万人去潜水。其中亚龙湾、蜈支洲岛、百福湾更是名气在外。

（本文选自百度百科词条“潜水”，有改动）

Recreational Diving

Recreational diving refers to diving activities for the purpose of underwater sightseeing and recreation. It is divided into snorkeling and scuba diving. Diving experiences are available at many seaside tourist attractions.

In scenic spots, tourists are usually guided by coaches to experience diving activities in the sea, and the depth usually does not exceed 12 meters. Even if you can't swim, you can enjoy diving. If you want to dive freely, you must have a diving license.

Sanya is a very famous diving resort in China, with 19 diving clubs and 26 diving spots, and more than 1 million people go there for diving every year. Yalong Bay, Wuzhizhou Island and Baifu Bay are the most famous place there.

第十课

您可以试试我们最新的SPA套餐

课前热身 Warming up

1. 你做过“SPA”吗？

   Have you ever done a SPA?

2. 请你说一说做“SPA”的流程。

   Could you tell us the procedure of doing a SPA?

课文 Text

李先生和李太太今天出门游玩，回到酒店后，李太太觉得有点儿累，想试试酒店的SPA、按摩服务。

Mr. Li and his wife went out for a trip today. After returning to the hotel, Mrs Li felt a little tired and wanted to try the SPA and massage services of the hotel.

Lǐ tàitai
李 太太

李伟的妻子

Liwei' wife

fúwùyuán
服务员

康体中心服务员

a waitress of the hotel fitness center

Fúwùyuán: Wǎnshang hǎo, huānyíng guānglín kāng tǐ zhōngxīn!
服务员：晚上 好，欢迎 光临 康 体 中心！

Lǐ tàitai: Nǐ hǎo, wǒ xiǎng zuò
李 太太：你 好，我 想 做 SPA。

Fúwùyuán: Hǎo de, zhè shì wǒmen de jiàgé dān, bù tóng de jīng yóu jiàgé
服务员：好 的，这 是 我们 的 价格 单，不 同 的 精 油 价格

bù yíyàng, nín xiǎng yào nǎ zhǒng ne?
不 一样，您 想 要 哪 种 呢？

Lǐ tàitai: Nǐmen zhèlǐ nǎ zhǒng bǐjiào hǎo ne?
李 太太：你们 这里 哪 种 比较 好 呢？

Fúwùyuán: Nín kěyǐ shì shi wǒmen zuì xīn de taocān, bāokuò
服务员：您可以试试我们最新的SPA套餐，包括60

fēn zhōng de shēntǐ jīng yóu ànmó hé fēn zhōng de miàn bù
分钟的身体精油按摩和90分钟的面部

hùlǐ, xiànzài hái kěyǐ dǎ bā zhé, fēicháng huásuàn。
护理，现在还可以打八折，非常划算。

Lǐ tàitai: Jiù zhège ba。
李太太：就这个吧。

Fúwùyuán: Qǐng nín gēn wǒ lái, jìshī mǎshàng jiù guòlái。
服务员：请您跟我来，技师马上就过来。

(sān fēn zhōng hòu)
（三分钟后）

Jìshī: Nín hǎo, ràng nín jiǔ děng le。Zhè shì nín de chá, hái yǒu ànmó
技师：您好，让您久等了。这是您的茶，还有按摩

fú, qǐng nín huàn hǎo yīfu hòu qiāo yi qiāo mén, wǒ jiù zài
服，请您换好衣服后敲一敲门，我就在

mén wài děnghòu。
门外等候。

(Lǐ tàitai huàn hǎo hòu)
（李太太换好后）

Jìshī: Qǐng nín pā zài chuáng shang。Ànmó de shíhou, kěnéng huì
技师：请您趴在床上。按摩的时候，可能会

yǒudiǎnr suāntòng, rúguǒ lìdù tài dà, nín kěyǐ gēn wǒ shuō。
有点儿酸痛，如果力度太大，您可以跟我说。

Lǐ tàitai: Hǎo de。
李太太：好的。

(ànmó zhōng)
(按摩 中)

Lǐ tàitai: Zhèlǐ lìdù kěyǐ dà yìdiǎnr。
李 太太:这里 力度 可以 大 一点儿。

Jìshī: Hǎo de。
技师:好 的。

Lǐ tàitai: Kěyǐ le, shāowēi qīng yìdiǎnr, yǒudiǎnr tòng。
李 太太:可以 了, 稍微 轻 一点儿,有点儿 痛。

Jìshī: Hǎo de。Zhèyàng kěyǐ ma?
技师:好 的。 这样 可以 吗?

Lǐ tàitai: Kěyǐ。
李 太太:可以。

(ànmó jiéshù)
(按摩 结束)

Jìshī: Tàitai, wǒ de fúwù jiéshù le。Nín kěyǐ zài zhèlǐ xiūxi yíxià。
技师:太太,我 的 服务 结束 了。您 可以 在 这里 休息 一下。

Zhèlǐ yǒu chá hé diǎnxin, nín kěyǐ xiǎngyòng。
这里 有 茶 和 点心, 您 可以 享用。

Lǐ tàitai: Hǎo de, xièxie nǐ!
李 太太:好 的,谢谢 你!

Jìshī: Bú kèqi, rúguǒ nín duì wǒ de fúwù gǎndào mǎnyì, qǐng nín zài
技师:不 客气,如果 您 对 我 的 服务 感到 满意, 请 您 在

wǒmen de fúwù dān shàng dǎ fēn, huānyíng xià cì zài lái。
我们 的 服务 单 上 打 分, 欢迎 下 次 再 来。

生词 New words

1	套餐	tàocān	名	package
2	不同	bù tóng		difference
3	精油	jīng yóu		essential oil
4	比较	bǐjiào	副	relatively
5	包括	bāokuò	动	to include
6	分钟	fēn zhōng		minute
7	身体	shēntǐ	名	body
8	面部护理	miàn bù hùlǐ		facial care
9	打折	dǎzhé	动	to discount
10	划算	huásuàn	形	budget-friendly
11	技师	jìshī	名	masseuse
12	久等	jiǔ děng		to wait for a long time
13	敲	qiāo	动	to knock
14	趴	pā	动	lie on one's stomach
15	酸痛	suāntòng	形	sore

16	力度	lìdù	名	strength
17	结束	jiéshù	动	to finish
18	休息	xiūxi	动	to rest
19	点心	diǎnxin	名	dim sum
20	享用	xiǎngyòng	动	enjoy
21	满意	mǎnyì	动	satisfaction
22	打分	dǎ fēn		rate

语言点 Language points

1. “不同……，……不一样”

different…, …is not the same

Bù tóng fángjiān, jiàgé bù yíyàng。
(1) 不同房间，价格不一样。

Bù tóng lóucéng, jiàgé bù yíyàng。
(2) 不同楼层，价格不一样。

Bù tóng yǒngchí, fēngjǐng bù yíyàng。
(3) 不同泳池，风景不一样。

2. “……后……”

...after...

Qǐng nín huàn hǎo yīfu hòu qiāo yi qiāo mén。
(1) 请 您 换 好 衣服 后 敲 一 敲 门。

Qǐng zài kèrén tuì fáng hòu dǎsǎo fángjiān。
(2) 请 在 客人 退 房 后 打扫 房间。

Wǒ quèrèn hòu gěi nín huífù。
(3) 我 确认 后 给 您 回复。

3. “有点儿……”

a little...

Tiānjì yǒngchí yǒudiǎnr lěng, háishì zài shì nèi ba。
(1) 天际 泳池 有点儿 冷，还是 在 室 内 吧。

Lìdù kěyǐ xiǎo yìdiǎnr ma, yǒudiǎnr tòng。
(2) 力度 可以 小 一点儿 吗，有点儿 痛。

Zhèxiē jiànshēn qìcái yǒudiǎnr jiù, qǐng nín zhùyì ānquán。
(3) 这些 健身 器材 有点儿 旧，请 您 注意 安全。

练习　Exercises

1. 看图片说词。

Speak out the words according to the pictures.

 (1) ________	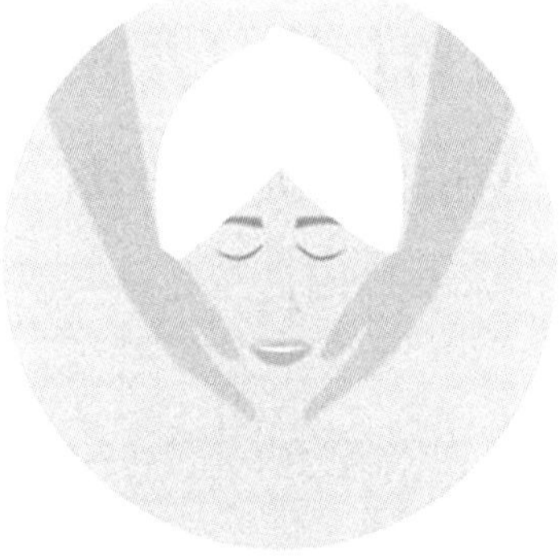 (2) ________
 (3) ________	 (4) ________

(5) ________________

(6) ________________

2. 短语连线，并完成句子。

Match the words and complete the sentences.

服务	享用	感到	打	精油	非常
八折	满意	结束	划算	点心	按摩

Nín shì wǒmen jiǔdiàn de lǎo kèhù, kěyǐ
(1) 您是我们酒店的老客户，可以________________。

Xiānsheng, wǒ de ________________ le, qǐng nín zài wǒmen de fúwù dān shang dǎ fēn。
(2) 先生，我的________________了，请您在我们的服务单上打分。

Ànmó hòu rúguǒ juéde è, kěyǐ zài zhèlǐ
(3) 按摩后如果觉得饿，可以在这里________________。

Rúguǒ nín duì wǒ de fúwù ________, huānyíng xià cì zài lái。
(4) 如果您对我的服务________，欢迎下次再来。

Nǐ kěyǐ shì shi wǒmen jiǔdiàn de ________ hé miàn bù hùlǐ。
(5) 你可以试试我们酒店的________和面部护理。

Rúguǒ nín tíqián yùdìng wǒmen jiǔdiàn de kèfáng kěyǐ huòdé miǎnfèi de SPA fúwù, ________。
(6) 如果您提前预订我们酒店的客房可以获得免费的SPA服务，________。

3. 根据要求，完成对话。

Complete the conversations.

(1) A: Nín hǎo, huānyíng guānglín ________!
A：您好，欢迎光临________！

B: Nín hǎo, wǒ xiǎng zuò SPA。
B：您好，我想做SPA。

A: Hǎo de, zhè shì wǒmen de ________, bù tóng de tàocān jiàgé bù yíyàng。
A：好的，这是我们的________，不同的套餐价格不一样。

B: Wǒ xiǎng zuò zuì xīn de SPA tàocān。
B：我想做最新的SPA套餐。

(2) A: Zhè shì nín de ________, nín huàn hǎo hòu, qǐng qiāo mén jiào wǒ。
A：这是您的________，您换好后，请敲门叫我。

B: Nín hǎo, wǒ de yīfu yǐjīng huàn hǎo le。
B：您好，我的衣服已经换好了。

A: Anmó de shíhou, kěnéng huì yǒudiǎnr suāntòng, ________,
A：按摩的时候，可能会有点儿酸痛，________，

nín kěyǐ gēn wǒ shuō。
您 可以 跟 我 说。

Hǎo de, xièxie nín。
B：好 的，谢谢 您。

4. 情景练习。

Practice speaking.

你是康体中心的 SPA 技师。今天的客人李先生是第一次做 SPA，请你向他介绍你们酒店的 SPA 套餐，询问他按摩的力度和效果。

You are a spa masseuse. The guest Mr. Li is doing spa for the first time today. Please introduce the spa package of your hotel to him and ask him about the strength and effect of your massage.

小知识 Notes

SPA 的魅力

SPA 是由专业技师、水、光线、精油、音乐等多个内容组合而成的舒缓减压方式，有减压、瘦身、美容等功效。

SPA 种类繁多，除了面部护理、身体护理、精油按摩、水疗沐浴等，还有亲亲鱼 SPA、红酒 SPA、巧克力 SPA、蛇疗 SPA 等。做 SPA 之前，可多喝水，为加强 SPA 的效果，也可以冲热水淋浴，让自己放松，享受 SPA 的按摩过程。

SPA 有多种套餐组合，费用也不等，一些 SPA 会馆会根据当地的消费水平制定价格。

（本文选自百度百科词条“SPA”，有改动）

The Charm of SPA

SPA is a soothing and stress-relieving treatment composed of professional therapists, water, light, essential oil, music, etc. It has the effects of reducing stress, slimming, improving skin conditions and so on.

There are many kinds of SPA. In addition to facial care, body care, essential oil massage, spa bath, there are also fish SPA, red wine SPA, chocolate SPA and snake therapy SPA. Before taking a SPA, you'd better drink plenty of water to enhance the effect of SPA. You can also take a hot shower to relax yourself and enjoy the massage process of SPA more.

There are a variety of SPA packages available, and the cost varies. Some SPA clubs set the prices according to the local consumption level.

参考答案

第一课

您好！请问有什么可以帮您

1.

酒店　房间　护照　邮件　姓名　早餐

2.

（1）您好！请问有什么可以帮您

（2）请问您要预订几号的房间

（3）请问您的护照号码是多少

（4）550 元一天

3.

答案合理即可，略。

第二课

欢迎您入住玫瑰酒店

1.

单人间　刷卡　美元　房卡　签名　高层

2

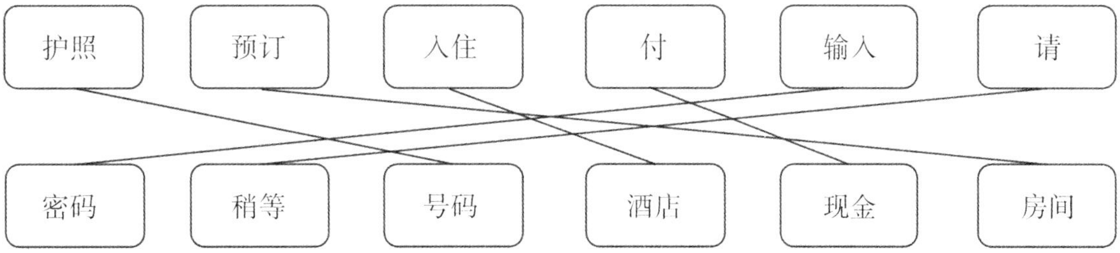

（1）预订房间

（2）护照号码

（3）请稍等

（4）入住酒店

（5）输入密码

（6）付现金

3.

答案合理即可，略。

第三课

您好！请填一下行李寄存单

1.

行李箱　出租车　寄存　住宿单　打印　门口

2.

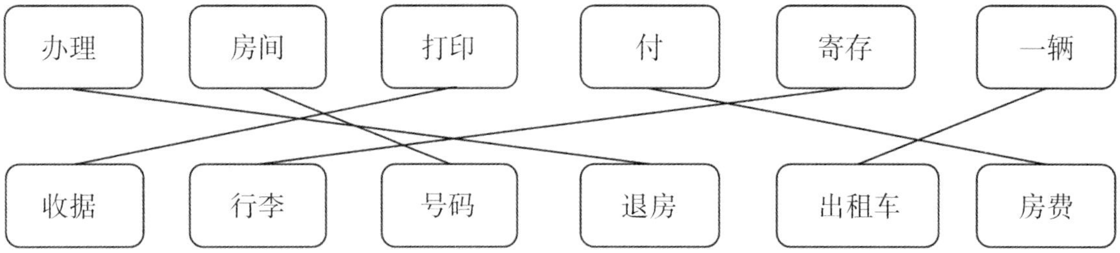

（1）办理退房

（2）房间号码

（3）寄存行李

（4）付房费

（5）打印收据

（6）一辆出租车

3.

（1）您的房间号码是多少

（2）请问您怎么付房费

（3）可以的，请您填一下行李寄存单

（4）需要给您叫一辆出租车吗

4.

答案合理即可，略。

第四课

您好！请问您需要订餐吗

1.

送餐　菜单　十点十分　汉堡　可乐　茶几

2.

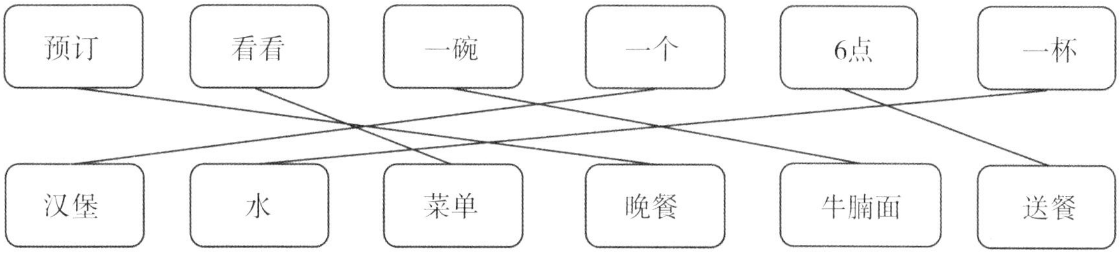

（1）预订晚餐

（2）一杯水

（3）一碗牛腩面

（4）一个汉堡

（5）看看菜单

（6）6 点送餐

3.

（1）您好，请问您需要订餐吗

（2）今天的牛排非常不错

（3）您要一碗牛腩面和一杯水

（4）6 点

4.

答案合理即可，略。

第五课

您好！请问您订位了吗

1.

餐厅　请坐　三明治　丰富　啤酒　汤

2.

（1）√　（2）×　（3）√　（4）√　（5）×

（6）×　（7）×

3.

答案合理即可，略。

第六课

可以为您打扫房间吗

1.

清扫牌　吸尘　毛巾　浴室　吹风机　吵

2.

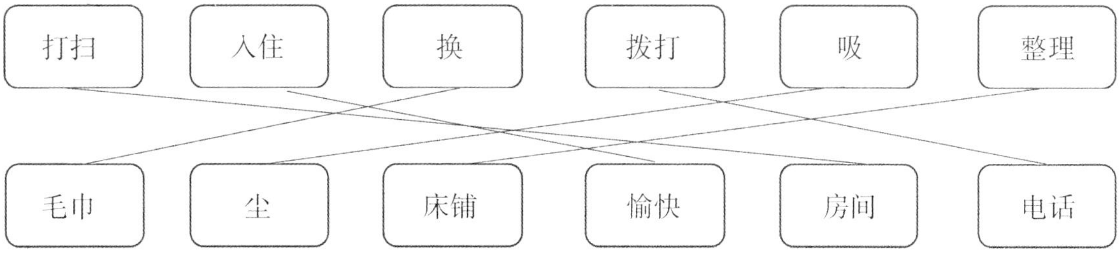

（1）吸尘

（2）打扫房间

（3）入住愉快

（4）换毛巾

（5）拨打电话

（6）整理床铺

3.

（1）可以为您打扫房间吗；半个小时左右就好了

（2）我让服务员给您送过来；可以给客房部打电话

4.

答案合理即可，略。

第七课

您有衣服要送洗吗

1.

裤子　衣服　衬衣　价格　抽屉　熨

2.

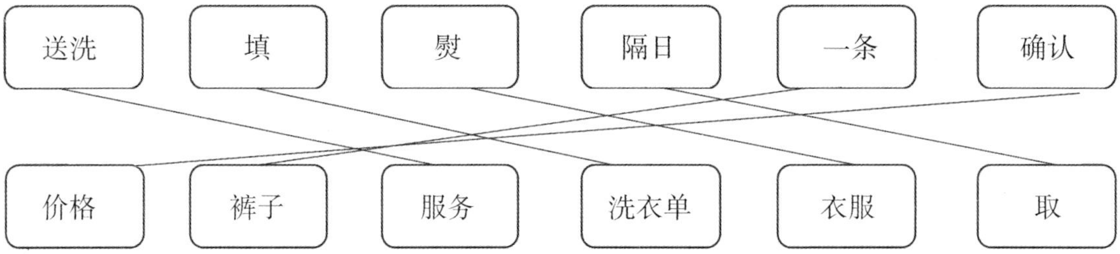

（1）一条裤子

（2）隔日取

（3）填洗衣单

（4）送洗服务

（5）熨衣服

（6）确认价格

3.

（1）您有衣服需要送洗吗；您能填一下洗衣单吗；抽屉里

（2）我们有快洗和隔日取；快洗的话，每件衣服 15 美元

4.

答案合理即可，略。

第八课

麻烦您登记一下房号和姓名

1.

跑步　房号　伸展　哑铃　跑步机　运动单车

2.

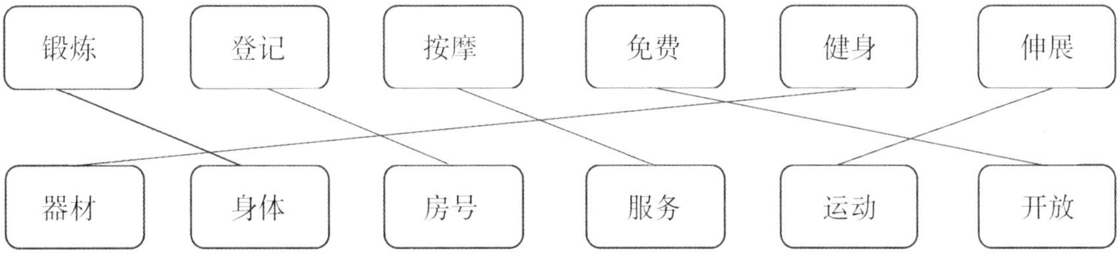

（1）登记房号

（2）免费开放

（3）健身器材

（4）锻炼身体

（5）按摩服务

（6）伸展运动

3.

（1）请问您想做什么运动呢；麻烦您先登记一下

（2）我们的健身房对酒店客人是免费开放的

4.

答案合理即可，略。

第九课

我们酒店有天际泳池

1.

天际泳池　泳帽　钥匙　照片　拍照　游客

2.

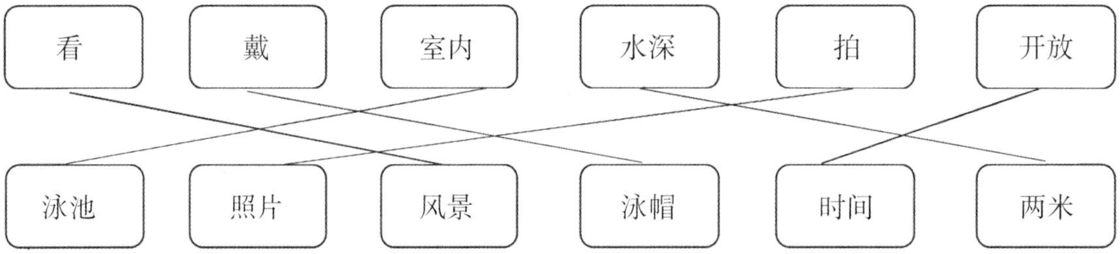

（1）看风景

（2）室内泳池

（3）拍照片

（4）戴泳帽

（5）水深两米

（6）开放时间

3.

（1）我们的天际泳池非常有名；最深的地方有两米

（2）室外泳池从早上 6 点到下午 6 点都开放，室内泳池开放时间是到晚上 9 点；室内泳池游泳要戴泳帽；您可以在我们中心购买

4.

答案合理即可，略。

第十课

您可以试试我们最新的 SPA 套餐

1.

点心　面部护理　技师　精油　休息　套餐

2.

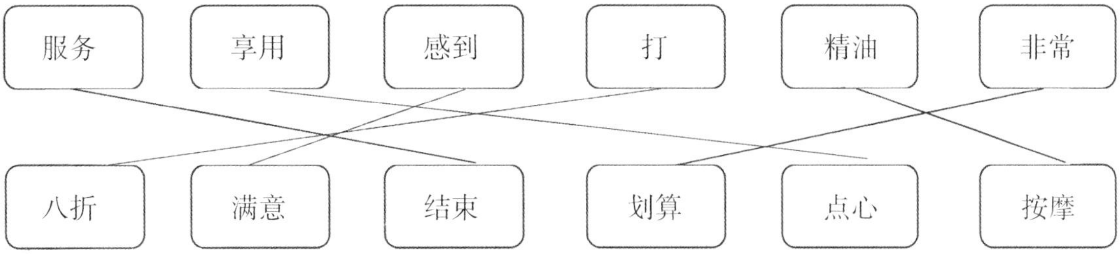

（1）打八折

（2）服务结束

（3）享用点心

（4）感到满意

（5）精油按摩

（6）非常划算

3.

（1）康体中心；价格单

（2）按摩服；如果力度太大

4.

答案合理即可，略。

附　录

附录一

汉语词类简称表
A List of Word Class Abbreviations

名词	míngcí	名	noun
代词	dàicí	代	pronoun
动词	dòngcí	动	verb
离合词	líhécí	动	separable verb
形容词	xíngróngcí	形	adjective
数词	shùcí	数	numeral
量词	liàngcí	量	measure word
数量词	shùliàngcí	数量	numeral-classifier phrase
副词	fùcí	副	adverb
介词	jiècí	介	preposition
连词	liáncí	连	conjunction
助词	zhùcí	助	particle

动态助词	dòngtài zhùcí		aspect particle
结构助词	jiégòu zhùcí		structural particle
语气助词	yǔqì zhùcí		modal particle
叹词	tàncí	叹	interjection
象声词	xiàngshēngcí	象	onomatopoeia
前缀	qiánzhuì		prefix
后缀	hòuzhuì		suffix

附录二

酒店汉语实用表达 80 句

Hotol Chinese Practical Expressions

Qǐngwèn nín yào yùdìng jǐ hào de fángjiān?
(1) 请问 您 要 预定 几 号 的 房间?

Qǐngwèn nín yào dān rén jiān háishi shuāng rén jiān?
(2) 请问 您 要 单 人 间 还是 双 人 间?

Dān rén jiān duōshao qián yìtiān?
(3) 单 人 间 多少 钱 一天?

Dān rén jiān měiyuán yìtiān, yǒu zǎocān。
(4) 单 人 间 88 美元 一天, 有 早餐。

Qǐngwèn nín yào zhù jǐ tiān?
(5) 请问 您 要 住 几 天?

Qǐng nín quèrèn yíxià。
(6) 请 您 确认 一下。

Qǐng gàosù wǒ nín de hùzhào xìngmíng、hùzhào hàomǎ hé yóuxiāng。
(7) 请 告诉 我 您 的 护照 姓名、护照 号码 和 邮箱。

Nín de fángjiān yùdìng hǎole。
(8) 您 的 房间 预订 好了。

Qǐngwèn hái yǒu shénme kěyǐ bāng nín ma?
(9) 请问 还 有 什么 可以 帮 您 吗?

Zhù nín shēnghuó yúkuài!
(10) 祝 您 生活 愉快!

Huānyíng lái dào Méigui jiǔdiàn。Huānyíng rùzhù Méigui jiǔdiàn。
(11) 欢迎 来 到 玫瑰 酒店。欢迎 入住 玫瑰 酒店。

Qǐngwèn yùdìng xìngmíng shì shénme?
(12) 请问 预订 姓名 是 什么?

Qǐng gěi wǒ nín de hùzhào。
(13) 请 给 我 您 的 护照。

Nín xūyào fù měiyuán yājīn。
(14) 您 需要 付 80 美元 押金。

Kěyǐ shuākǎ, yě kěyǐ fù xiànjīn。
(15) 可以 刷卡, 也 可以 付 现金。

Bùhǎoyìsi, xiānsheng, zhǐ néng yòng měiyuán。
(16) 不好意思, 先生, 只 能 用 美元。

Qǐng shūrù mìmǎ。Qǐng zài zhèlǐ qiānmíng。
(17) 请 输入 密码。请 在 这里 签名。

Nín de fángjiān shì zhè shì nín de fángkǎ。
(18) 您 的 房间 是 1208, 这 是 您 的 房卡。

Wǒ yào bànlǐ tuì fáng。
(19) 我 要 办理 退 房。

Qǐngwèn nín de fángjiān hàomǎ shì duōshao?
(20) 请问 您 的 房间 号码 是 多少?

Fángfèi shì měiyuán yìtiān, yígòng shì měiyuán。
(21) 房费 是 88 美元 一天, 一共 是 246 美元。

Wǒ xūyào fángfèi shōujù hé zhùsù dān, kěyǐ dǎyìn gěi wǒ ma?
(22) 我 需要 房费 收据 和 住宿 单, 可以 打印 给 我 吗?

Qǐngwèn, zhèlǐ kěyǐ jìcún xíngli ma?
(23) 请问, 这里 可以 寄存 行李 吗?

Qǐng nín tián yíxià xíngli jìcún dān。
(24) 请 您 填 一下 行李 寄存 单。

Nín píng xíngli dān jiù kěyǐ ná xíngli。
(25) 您 凭 行李 单 就 可以 拿 行李。

Xūyào gěi nín jiào yí liàng chūzūchē ma?
(26) 需要 给 您 叫 一 辆 出租车 吗?

Zhèlǐ shì cānyǐn bù, qǐngwèn nín xūyào dìng cān ma?
(27) 这里 是 餐饮 部, 请问 您 需要 订 餐 吗?

Nín yào sòng cān háishi dào cāntīng chī ne?
(28) 您 要 送 餐 还是 到 餐厅 吃呢?

Wǎncān càidān fàng zài chájī shang, nín kěyǐ kàn kan。
(29) 晚餐 菜单 放 在 茶几 上, 您 可以 看 看。

Jīntiān wǎncān de zhǔshí shì miànshí, niúnǎn miàn de wèidào fēicháng búcuò, nín kěyǐ shì shi。
(30) 今天 晚餐 的 主食 是 面食, 牛腩 面 的 味道 非常 不错, 您 可以 试 试。

Hái yào bié de ma?
(31) 还 要 别 的 吗?

Qǐngwèn sūdá shuǐ jiā bīng ma?
(32) 请问 苏打 水 加 冰 吗?

Wǎncān huì zài diǎn dào diǎn bàn zhī jiān sòng dào nín de fángjiān。
(33) 晚餐 会 在6 点 到6 点 半 之 间 送 到 您 的 房间。

Nín de wǎncān yǐjīng yùdìng chénggōng。
(34) 您 的 晚餐 已经 预定 成功。

Nín hǎo, huānyíng guānglín! Qǐngwèn nín dìngwèi le ma?
(35) 您 好, 欢迎 光临! 请问 您 订位 了 吗?

Xiānsheng, qǐngwèn nín jǐ wèi ne?
(36) 先生, 请问 您 几 位 呢?

Xiānsheng, zuò zài zhèlǐ kěyǐ ma?
(37) 先生, 坐 在 这里 可以 吗?

Xiānsheng, qǐng zuò! Zhè shì càidān, nín kěyǐ kàn kan。
(38) 先生, 请 坐! 这 是 菜单, 您 可以 看 看。

Xiānsheng, jīntiān de wǎncān fēicháng fēngfù, nín xiǎng chī diǎnr shénme ne?
(39) 先生, 今天 的 晚餐 非常 丰富, 您 想 吃 点儿 什么 呢?

Jīntiān de niúpái fēicháng xīnxiān, nín kěyǐ shì shi。
(40) 今天 的 牛排 非常 新鲜, 您 可以 试 试。

Niúpái nín yào jǐ chéng shú?
(41) 牛排 您 要 几 成 熟?

Yǐnliào huòzhě jiǔ xūyào ma?
(42) 饮料 或者 酒 需要 吗?

Xiānsheng, qǐng shāo děng yíhuìr。 Nín de cài fēn zhōng zuǒyòu sòng lái。
(43) 先生, 请 稍 等 一会儿。您 的 菜 30 分 钟 左右 送 来。

Qǐngwèn xūyào dǎsǎo fángjiān ma?
(44) 请问 需要 打扫 房间 吗?

Rúguǒ nín xiàwǔ xūyào dǎsǎo fángjiān, qǐng bōdǎ yǔ kèfáng bù liánxì。
(45) 如果 您 下午 需要 打扫 房间, 请 拨打“5”与 客房 部 联系。

Zhèxiē máojīn hái yào yòng ma?
(46) 这些 毛巾 还 要 用 吗?

Xūyào xiànzài gěi nín xī chén ma?
(47) 需要 现在 给 您 吸 尘 吗?

Qǐngwèn xūyào bāng nín zhěnglǐ chuángpù ma?
(48) 请问 需要 帮 您 整理 床铺 吗?

Wǒ děng huìr gěi nín sòng lái。
(49) 我 等 会儿 给 您 送 来。

Nín yǒu yīfu yào sòng xǐ ma?
(50) 您 有 衣服 要 送 洗 吗?

Nín néng tián yíxià xǐ yī dān ma?
(51) 您 能 填 一下 洗 衣 单 吗?

Nín kěyǐ zài xǐ yī dān shàng xiě míng nǎ jiàn yīfu xūyào yùn。
(52) 您 可以 在 洗 衣 单 上 写 明 哪 件 衣服 需要 熨。

Wǒmen yǒu kuài xǐ hé gérì qǔ, nín xūyào nǎ zhǒng ne?
(53) 我们 有 快 洗 和 隔日 取, 您 需要 哪 种 呢?

Kuài xǐ de huà, měi jiàn yīfu měiyuán。
(54) 快 洗 的 话, 每 件 衣服 15 美元。

Zhǐyào ge xiǎoshí jiù hǎole。
(55) 只要 3 个 小时 就 好了。

Nín yígòng sòng xǐ jiàn yīfu, wǒmen huì zài míngtiān shàngwǔ diǎn zhīqián sòng huí。
（56）您一共送洗3件衣服，我们会在明天上午8点之前送回。

Huānyíng guānglín kāng tǐ zhōngxīn。
（57）欢迎光临康体中心。

Wǒmen jiǔdiàn de kāng tǐ zhōngxīn yǒu jiànshēnfáng hé yóuyǒngchí, hái yǒu sāngná hé ànmó fúwù。
（58）我们酒店的康体中心有健身房和游泳池，还有桑拿和按摩服务。

Qǐngwèn nín xiǎng zuò shénme yùndòng ne?
（59）请问您想做什么运动呢？

Máfan nín xiān dēngjì yíxià fánghào hé xìngmíng。
（60）麻烦您先登记一下房号和姓名。

Wǒmen de jiànshēnfáng duì jiǔdiàn kèrén shì miǎnfèi de。
（61）我们的健身房对酒店客人是免费的。

Shǐyòng qián zuìhǎo xiān zuò shēnzhǎn yùndòng。
（62）使用前最好先做伸展运动。

Rúguǒ nín yǒu shénme wèntí, kěyǐ suíshí jiào wǒ。
（63）如果您有什么问题，可以随时叫我。

Wǒ hěn lèyì wèi nín fúwù。
（64）我很乐意为您服务。

Wǒmen jiǔdiàn yǒu yí gè shì nèi héngwēn yǒngchí hé yí gè shì wài tiānjì yǒngchí。
（65）我们酒店有一个室内恒温泳池和一个室外天际泳池。

Wǒmen de tiānjì yǒngchí fēicháng yǒumíng, jīngcháng yǒu yóukè lái pāizhào。
（66）我们的天际泳池非常有名，经常有游客来拍照。

Zuì shēn de dìfang yǒu liǎng mǐ。
（67）最深的地方有两米。

Zài shì nèi yǒngchí yóuyǒng de hua yào dài shàng yǒngmào。
(68) 在室内 泳池 游泳 的话 要 戴 上 泳帽。

Nín kěyǐ zài wǒmen zhōngxīn gòumǎi, kuài qián yì dǐng。
(69) 您可以在 我们 中心 购买，30 块 钱 一 顶。

Wǎng qián zǒu jiùshì gēngyīshì, zhè shì yàoshi。
(70) 往 前 走 就是 更衣室，这 是 钥匙。

Bù tóng de jīng yóu jiàgé bù yíyàng。
(71) 不 同 的 精 油 价格 不 一样。

Jìshī mǎshàng jiù guòlái。
(72) 技师 马上 就 过来。

Qǐng nín huàn hǎo yīfu hòu qiāo yi qiāo mén, wǒ jiù zài mén wài děnghòu。
(73) 请 您 换 好 衣服 后 敲 一 敲 门，我 就 在 门 外 等候。

Qǐng nín pā zài chuáng shàng。
(74) 请 您 趴 在 床 上。

Ànmó de shíhou, kěnéng huì yǒudiǎnr suāntòng。
(75) 按摩 的 时候，可能 会 有点儿 酸痛。

Rúguǒ lìdù tài dà, nín kěyǐ gēn wǒ shuō。
(76) 如果 力度 太 大，您 可以 跟 我 说。

Zhèlǐ lìdù kěyǐ dà yìdiǎnr。
(77) 这里 力度 可以 大 一点儿。

Wǒ de fúwù jiéshù le。
(78) 我 的 服务 结束 了。

Zhèlǐ yǒu chá hé diǎnxin, nín kěyǐ xiǎngyòng。
(79) 这里 有 茶 和 点心，您 可以 享用。

Rúguǒ nín duì wǒ de fúwù gǎndào mǎnyì, qǐng nín zài wǒmen de fúwù dān shang dǎ fēn。
(80) 如果 您 对 我 的 服务 感到 满意，请 您 在 我们 的 服务 单 上 打 分。

附录三

词汇表 Glossary*

生词总表
（按音序排列）

A

按摩	ànmó	（8）

B

办理	bànlǐ	（3）
帮	bāng	（1）
包括	bāokuò	（10）
杯	bēi	（4）
比较	bǐjiào	（10）
拨打	bōdǎ	（6）
不同	bù tóng	（10）

C

菜单	càidān	（4）

* （ ）括号里的数字表示生词所在的课。

餐厅	cāntīng	(2)
餐饮部	cānyǐn bù	(4)
层	céng	(2)
茶几	chájī	(4)
查	chá	(2)
吵	chǎo	(6)
衬衣	chènyī	(7)
吃	chī	(5)
抽屉	chōuti	(7)
出门	chūmén	(6)
出行	chūxíng	(3)
出租车	chūzūchē	(3)
床单	chuángdān	(6)
床铺	chuángpù	(6)
吹风机	chuīfēngjī	(6)

D

打分	dǎ fēn	(10)
打扫	dǎsǎo	(6)
打印	dǎyìn	(3)
打折	dǎzhé	(10)
带	dài	(3)
戴	dài	(9)
单	dān	(3)
当然	dāngrán	(7)

登记	dēngjì	(8)
点	diǎn	(5)
点心	diǎnxin	(10)
顶	dǐng	(9)
订餐	dìng cān	(4)
订位	dìngwèi	(5)
锻炼	duànliàn	(8)

F

房费	fángfèi	(3)
房间	fángjiān	(1)
房卡	fángkǎ	(2)
非常	fēicháng	(2)
分钟	fēn zhōng	(10)
份	fèn	(5)
丰富	fēngfù	(5)
风景	fēngjǐng	(9)
服务	fúwù	(7)
付	fù	(2)

G

感谢	gǎnxiè	(2)
高	gāo	(2)
隔日	gérì	(7)
给	gěi	(2)

跟	gēn	(5)
关门	guānmén	(9)

H

还是	háishi	(1)
汉堡	hàn bǎo	(4)
号码	hàomǎ	(1)
恒温	héngwēn	(9)
护照	hùzhào	(1)
划算	huásuàn	(10)
欢迎	huānyíng	(2)
换	huàn	(6)
或者	huòzhě	(5)

J

寄存	jìcún	(3)
技师	jìshī	(10)
加冰	jiā bīng	(4)
价格	jiàgé	(7)
检查	jiǎnchá	(7)
件	jiàn	(7)
健身房	jiànshēnfáng	(8)
结束	jiéshù	(10)
结算	jiésuàn	(4)
精油	jīng yóu	(10)

久等	jiǔ děng	(10)
酒店	jiǔdiàn	(1)

K

康体中心	kāng tǐ zhōngxīn	(8)
靠窗	kào chuāng	(5)
裤子	kùzi	(7)
快洗	kuài xǐ	(7)

L

乐意	lèyì	(8)
力度	lìdù	(10)
辆	liàng	(3)

M

麻烦	máfan	(6)
马上	mǎshàng	(5)
满意	mǎnyì	(10)
毛巾	máojīn	(6)
每	měi	(7)
美元	měiyuán	(1)
门口	ménkǒu	(3)
密码	mìmǎ	(2)
免费	miǎnfèi	(8)
面部护理	miàn bù hùlǐ	(10)

N

拿	ná	(2)
牛腩面	niúnǎn miàn	(4)

P

趴	pā	(10)
拍照	pāizhào	(9)
跑步	pǎobù	(8)
跑步机	pǎobùjī	(8)
啤酒	píjiǔ	(5)
凭	píng	(3)

Q

器材	qìcái	(8)
签名	qiānmíng	(2)
钱	qián	(1)
浅水区	qiǎn shuǐ qū	(9)
敲	qiāo	(10)
请问	qǐngwèn	(1)
取	qǔ	(7)
确认	quèrèn	(1)

R

认真	rènzhēn	(7)
入住	rùzhù	(2)

S

三明治	sānmíngzhì	(5)
桑拿	sāngná	(8)
沙拉	shālā	(5)
稍等	shāo děng	(2)
稍后	shāohòu	(1)
伸展	shēnzhǎn	(8)
身体	shēntǐ	(10)
生活	shēnghuó	(1)
时间	shíjiān	(6)
试	shì	(9)
室内	shì nèi	(9)
室外	shì wài	(9)
收到	shōu dào	(1)
收据	shōujù	(3)
输入	shūrù	(2)
熟	shú	(5)
刷卡	shuākǎ	(2)
水深	shuǐ shēn	(9)
送餐	sòng cān	(4)
苏打水	sūdá shuǐ	(4)
酸痛	suāntòng	(10)
随时	suíshí	(8)

T

汤	tāng	(5)
套餐	tàocān	(10)
提供	tígōng	(7)
体验	tǐyàn	(8)
天	tiān	(1)
天际	tiānjì	(9)
填	tián	(3)
听说	tīngshuō	(8)
推荐	tuījiàn	(4)
退房	tuì fáng	(3)

W

晚餐	wǎncān	(4)
碗	wǎn	(4)
网红	wǎng hóng	(9)
往	wǎng	(9)
位子	wèizi	(5)
味道	wèidào	(4)

X

吸尘	xī chén	(6)
洗	xǐ	(7)
洗衣单	xǐ yī dān	(7)
喜欢	xǐhuan	(2)

现金	xiànjīn	(2)
限制	xiànzhì	(8)
箱	xiāng	(3)
享用	xiǎngyòng	(10)
小票	xiǎopiào	(2)
新	xīn	(6)
新鲜	xīnxiān	(5)
行李	xíngli	(3)
姓名	xìngmíng	(1)
休息	xiūxi	(10)
需要	xūyào	(2)

Y

押金	yājīn	(2)
哑铃	yǎlíng	(8)
钥匙	yàoshi	(9)
一共	yígòng	(3)
衣服	yīfu	(7)
饮料	yǐnliào	(5)
应该	yīnggāi	(6)
泳池	yǒngchí	(9)
泳帽	yǒng mào	(9)
用	yòng	(2)
邮件	yóujiàn	(1)
游客	yóukè	(9)

游泳池	yóuyǒngchí	(8)
有名	yǒumíng	(9)
愉快	yúkuài	(1)
浴室	yùshì	(6)
预订	yùdìng	(1)
运动单车	yùndòng dānchē	(8)
熨	yùn	(7)

Z

再	zài	(4)
早餐	zǎocān	(1)
这里	zhèlǐ	(1)
枕套	zhěntào	(6)
之间	zhī jiān	(4)
之前	zhīqián	(7)
只能	zhǐ néng	(2)
只要	zhǐyào	(7)
主食	zhǔshí	(4)
住	zhù	(1)
住宿	zhùsù	(3)
祝	zhù	(1)
最	zuì	(8)
坐	zuò	(5)

专有名词

李伟	Lǐ Wěi	(1)
曼谷	Màngǔ	(1)
玫瑰酒店	Méigui Jiǔdiàn	(1)